Faith Matters

Carol Round

Buoy Up
Press

Denton, Texas

Buoy Up Press
An imprint of AWOC.COM Publishing
P.O. Box 2819
Denton, TX 76202

Manufactured in the United States of America

ISBN: 978-0-937660-83-6

Table of Contents

Acknowledgements

"I am convinced beyond a shadow of any doubt that the most valuable pursuit we can embark upon is to know God." –Kay Arthur

I have been on a quest to know God since I realized that He is the missing piece of this puzzle we call life. Without Him, life just does not make sense. Without Him, I could not have survived—with grace—the life-changing events I have faced since Jesus began knocking at the door of my heart. Before I said, "Come in, Jesus," He knew what I would encounter and what is yet to come. However, with His strength, I can face each new day and say, "This is the day that the Lord has made. I will rejoice and be glad in it."

I rejoice in the blessings of my friendships with women of faith who, like me, realize that "Faithful friends are beyond price; no amount can balance their worth."–*Bible (Old Testament) Sirach 6:15 NRSV*

I count among my faithful and faith-filled friends the following women and dedicate this volume to them. In no particular order, for they are all equal in His eyes and mine:

Charlie Shotsky, Clarice Doyle, Melissa Holt, Sharon Brown, Janelle Brammer, Dorothy Willman, Sharon Koons, Jennifer Kirby, Roma Estes, Mary Lou Peterson, Ceanne Brunk, Maridel Stout, Audrey Folsom, Jackie Golden, Barbara Beck and Jeanette Standfield

Whatever You Do

"Whatever you do, work at it with all your heart, as working for the Lord, not for men, since you know that you will receive an inheritance from the Lord as a reward. It is the Lord Christ you are serving."
Colossians 3:23-24

Like most people today, I have many household conveniences: a dishwasher, a microwave, a washer and a dryer. We have come to believe, however, that they are necessities. Sometimes I like doing things the old-fashioned way.

Six years ago, when my son and his wife lived in Texas, I made the 650 mile round trip several times a year to visit. While the two were at work, I found more pleasure in doing their household chores than I did in checking out the local tourist attractions.

They were lacking one convenience and another was broken. The rental house where they lived did not have a dishwasher and their clothes dryer needed repairs. I had forgotten how soothing it was to look out the kitchen window as I stood at the sink to wash and then dry the dishes by hand.

I also enjoyed hanging their freshly laundered clothes in the hot Texas sun. Using old-fashioned wooden clothespins, I hung towels, sheets, and assorted items of their wardrobe on a line strung between two poles in their backyard. It didn't take long for the July heat to dry each one, leaving a fresh smell that no dryer sheet can duplicate.

Each simple act was a reminder of the need to slow down and not only savor the moment but enjoy that time to reflect and communicate with our Savior. In spite of all our modern conveniences, our society as a whole isn't content. I think it is because our microwave–nuke it and get it done–society has forgotten the pleasure that can be found in the simple things in life.

I didn't spend much time indoors watching television when I was a child. I still don't. Whether it was building tents out of quilts on my mother's clothesline or playing with bugs, I found joy in the small things.

Recently, after reading a newspaper article about the work ethic of today's youth, I had a discussion with a friend about that topic. We both agreed that our generation had been raised with moral values that taught us the importance of work and its inherent ability to strengthen character. In addition to teaching us about responsibility, we learned the significance of duty and self-discipline.

A chapter in "The Purpose Driven Life" discusses our attitudes about what we do, whether it is running a large corporation or taking out the trash. Brother Lawrence, a seventh century cook in a French monastery, wrote "Practicing the Presence of God". He turned commonplace tasks, like preparing meals and washing dishes, into acts of praise and communion with God. Instead of doing it for yourself, he says, we should begin doing it for God.

Even the mundane, everyday tasks can bring pleasure if we can remember that we are doing it for Him.

Dirty Dishes in the Sink

"...always giving thanks to God the Father for everything, in the name of our Lord Jesus Christ."
Ephesians 5:20

As I washed the round metal pan, I realized that it had been a week since I had used it to serve pizza to a friend who had visited for lunch. One of my first thoughts was, "I'm way too busy."

I also thought about my mother's teachings. She was a stay-at-home mom who cooked meals from scratch and sewed all of her daughters' clothing. I never remember her leaving dirty dishes in the sink. She reared her daughters to believe that you just didn't do that. Neither did you serve frozen food from a box.

Cooking has never really been "my thing." I know my way around the kitchen. I can follow a simple recipe and my food hasn't killed anyone, yet. Although I learned to cook from scratch in high school home economics classes, I prefer spending less time in the kitchen. I was excited when Betty Crocker came on the scene with almost-instant mixes and canned frosting.

For holidays like Thanksgiving, Christmas and Easter, I do fix a turkey or ham with all the trimmings. My first attempt at baking a turkey proved that, although I was my mother's daughter, we were not cut out of the same cloth. No one had ever bothered to inform me that you were supposed to reach up inside the stupid bird and remove the giblets. Why on earth, I thought later, would they do that?

When I removed my first turkey, golden-brown and oozing with juices, from the oven, I was certainly proud of myself. When I went to carve the turkey, I cut into something mushy. It was the plastic bag holding the giblets.

I love giblet gravy but I wasn't about to use the sticky innards to prepare the Thanksgiving treat. Although we didn't have anything to enhance the taste of the mashed potatoes, we still enjoyed our usual traditional meal.

As blessed people, we sometimes forget that dirty dishes in the sink are actually a sign of prosperity. I received a letter in the mail today from John 3:16 Mission, a ministry established in Tulsa in 1952. Two years ago, I began contributing to their outreach to the homeless. Providing around 40,000 meals at Thanksgiving for the hungry and the hurting, the nonprofit organization relies on donations to make that mission possible.

Matthew 25:35 reminds us that the Lord blesses us so that we can be a blessing to others. It is a call to action: "...I was hungry and you gave me food; I was thirsty and you gave me drink; I was a stranger and you took me in; I was naked and you clothed me; I was in prison and you came to me."

When we see others in need, let it be a reminder that our abundant blessings should be used for God's glory. As we take inventory of what He has provided us, then our hands should reach out to help provide hope for others.

Have a Hundred-Dollar Holiday

"Then he said to them, 'Watch out! Be on your guard against all kinds of greed; a man's life does not consist in the abundance of his possessions.'" *Luke 12:15*

If you ask any American child what he likes about Christmas, you would probably hear the same answer. In their excitement, most would probably shout the word "presents" or "toys."

Ask any harried parent what he likes about Christmas and I believe you would get a different answer. You would get even another viewpoint if you asked retailers.

The holiday season is upon us. Although the advertising blitz has been going on for a few months— or at least it feels that way—I find it hard to get excited. I don't think I am alone.

If you asked me to describe the perfect holiday season, I would include the following: the company of loved ones, good food, fun and relaxation, and maybe a few inches of snow. Although my wish list seems simple, for many, this ideal could not be farther from reality.

Too often, the holidays seem to exhaust us because we feel trapped by the shopping, spending, and frenzied preparations when we should feel uplifted. A recent national survey revealed that 70 percent of Americans long for less emphasis on gift giving and spending.

In his 1998 book titled *Hundred Dollar Holiday: The Case for a More Joyful Christmas*, Bill McKibben offers a simple proposal in the midst of the holiday madness. He suggests spending only $100 (total) on Christmas, and instead of shopping, we should spend time with the people we love.

Critics of McKibben have called him the grinch that stole Christmas. Responding to the criticism, McKibben said, "I've been called my share of names, but the only one that ever really stung was 'grinch.'"

It was with apprehension that McKibben picked up his daughter's well-worn copy of the Dr. Seuss classic and reread the popular tale. After rereading the story, McKibben found new understanding.

In Seuss's book, the Grinch hears the sound of singing on Christmas morning and realizes he has not stopped Christmas at all.

And the Grinch, with his grinch-feet ice-cold in the snow.
Stood puzzling and puzzling: "How could it be so?
It came without ribbons! It came without tags!
"It came without packages, boxes or bags!"
And he puzzled three hours, `till his puzzler was sore.
Then the Grinch thought of something he hadn't before!
"Maybe Christmas," he thought, "doesn't come from a store.
"Maybe Christmas... perhaps... means a little bit more!"

Wouldn't it be nice if more people realized that Christmas doesn't come from a store and is maybe... perhaps... a little bit more?

In a society, where material goods are bountiful but quality time is not, I think McKibben has a great idea. If we start putting the 'peace of mind' back into Christmas, with a spending limit, we will find, just like the Grinch, that the true meaning of Christmas was right under our noses the whole time.

As you make your holiday shopping list, remember the old cliché, "Jesus is the reason for the season."

All I Want for Christmas

"Worship the Lord with gladness; come before him with joyful songs." *Psalm 100:2*

One of the things I love about the Christmas season is the joyful songs. I have my favorites, from the spiritual to the secular. However, I've never been able to sing *a cappella*. But with loud musical accompaniment, I don't sound too bad.

When I was about 8-years-old, I was part of an all-school Christmas program. One of the popular songs at that time was "All I Want for Christmas is My Two Front Teeth." I was one of three who had missing front teeth. Our role was to grin big when the rest of the elementary chorus that was performing for parents, relatives and friends sang that line. The audience could see the gap in the front of our mouths where our permanent teeth had not yet appeared.

Sometimes, however, there are things missing in our lives that are not as apparent. Recently, I was reading a newspaper article titled "Family that gives could use some help," about a single mother who wanted her two daughters to remember the reason for celebrating Christmas. She didn't want them to focus on the gifts.

The 32-year-old mom has started a family tradition of donating in some small way during the holiday season. She, along with her two daughters, bakes cookies for needy families. They also volunteer at their church and collect items for food drives.

The article quoted the young mother: "The whole purpose of Christmas goes to doing something for someone else. It's about how God gave his son to die for us. So, we always give away something or volunteer somewhere."

That may not seem amazing until you read the rest of the story. The writer revealed that the young mother needed help to provide a modest Christmas for her girls. She said, "My girls have never wanted name-brand things. They are happy with whatever they are given. They are happy with little stuff."

The mother, who frugally manages her paycheck to make ends meet during the year, has applied to the Salvation Army to help fulfill her daughter's Christmas wish list. Neither girl has a list of toys. Her oldest daughter has asked for one thing—a new Bible.

December is especially difficult for the family. Because the girls are out of school for the holidays, there are additional costs for heating and food, putting a squeeze on an already strapped budget.

"When December comes," says the young mother, "my money is gone. I just can't make it through."

Through the Salvation Army Angel Tree project, the young family will receive help this Christmas. The young mother is just thankful for the ability to focus on the spiritual aspect of the holiday and not worry about bills. Even during tough financial times, this family is willing to give to others in need. In return, they do not ask for much.

I was touched by this story. It was a wonderful reminder that "All I want for Christmas" is to be a blessing to others. What about you?

Egg on the Ceiling

"Blessed is the man who perseveres under trial, because when he has stood the test, he will receive the crown of life that God has promised to those who love him." *James 1:12*

Since I am single, I don't find myself cooking too many meals. It's too much trouble to mess up the kitchen for one.

Although I don't mind preparing food for family and friends, cooking has never been my forte. Both of my grandmothers and my mother were excellent cooks, especially my maternal grandmother. If you had led me blindfolded into her kitchen, I would have known from the tantalizing smells that it was my grandmother Beulah's domain. She was known for her feather-light gingerbread and her carrot cake.

When I was a teenager, I took cooking classes. One of my signature specialties was key lime pie. After tasting a sample, my grandmother requested the recipe. I hand copied the ingredients and directions on a 3 x 5 card. Later that week, my grandmother phoned my mother. In tears, she said, "Ruby, I have stirred and stirred the filling for Carol's pie but it won't turn green."

It was only after a brief question and answer session that my mother discovered I had omitted one important step. I had forgotten to include the fact that you must add several drops of green food coloring to acquire the correct tint.

I've had my own share of cooking disasters, including the time I let a pot of eggs boil dry. I was going to devil the eggs for Thanksgiving. Busy with other preparations for the holiday, I forgot about the boiling water until I heard several loud explosions. When I finally detected the source of the sound, I found egg splattered all over my kitchen. Scraping the minute fragments of egg from the textured ceiling is not easy.

Sometimes life can be like that—as difficult as cleaning egg from the ceiling. I recently had the opportunity to visit with a young man who had been kicked out of his parents' home almost 10 years ago. Kenny's road has been bumpy. Until a business owner took an interest in helping the young man, Kenny would sometimes find himself sleeping in a car when he didn't have a friend with whom to stay. Kenny, however, has persevered, and is now the general manager of four fast food restaurants.

"I'm not perfect," he says. "I've not always been a good kid but I had an opportunity to change my life and I did. I chose to learn from my mistakes."

I was inspired by this young man who has turned his life around. He could have easily gone down the wrong path if it had not been for a benevolent man who saw the promise in a 16-year-old and offered him a job.

During this holiday season, let's not forget those who are less fortunate, the ones who need a helping hand. Look for the promise in each human that our heavenly Father saw when He came to earth as our Savior over 2,000 years ago.

A Wonderful Life Worth Living

"I wish that all men were as I am. But each man has his own gift from God; one has this gift, another has that." 1 Corinthians 7:7

I turned 54 last month. I'm not afraid to admit my age, because as I told someone recently, with age, life just gets better. While younger people might find that amusing, they still have much to learn.

In my 40s, I began to question many things about my life, including the realization that my life was probably close to being half over. I don't like to look at the glass as half empty. Like my life, I prefer to think of the glass as half full—and the best is yet to come. However, a recent six-week study at our church made me realize that I was still thirsty for more. I want my glass completely full and running over.

In "Treasures of the Transformed Life: Satisfying Your Soul's Thirst for More," John Ed Mathison talks about our need for more. In today's society, we have so many choices that life can be downright confusing. However, no matter how good life is, we thirst for more. Sometimes we don't really know what is missing.

We long for a more fulfilling life, one rich with meaning and joy. We can seek it in material things, but the satisfaction that we get is as fleeting as snowflakes that melt when they hit warm concrete.

In the classic Christmas movie, "It's a Wonderful Life," Jimmy Stewart plays George Bailey. Due to a series of circumstances, George has settled for life in his small hometown, instead of going off to see the world. One Christmas Eve, George attempts suicide because he thinks he is a failure. He wishes he had never been born. George gains the attention of Clarence, his guardian angel, sent to help him in his hour of need. The movie, told through flashbacks, reveals the people whose lives have been touched by George and the difference he has made to the community in which he lives.

"Strange, isn't it?" says Clarence. "Each man's life touches so many other lives. When he isn't around he leaves an awful hole, doesn't he?"

Clarence is right. We leave an awful hole when we don't live our lives according to God's plan. Not only do we shortchange ourselves, but we also miss God's best for our lives. Our lives, no matter how rich with blessings, are never complete until we realize we were born to give ourselves away. As Mathison says, "I'm talking about giving of yourself, your time, and your talents, just for the joy of knowing it was what you were created to do."

During separate conversations with two different individuals recently, I experienced what I call, God moments. During the course of our discussions, we realized that God had brought us together for a reason. Humbled by God's awesome plan, I shivered because I could see God's fingerprints all over my life—and it's a wonderful life worth living.

Are you living your life for Him?

The Eternal Christmas Gift

"For God so loved the world that he gave his one and only Son, that whoever believes in him shall not perish but have eternal life." *John 3:16*

What adult can't remember their childhood years and being excited about Christmas morning? I recall the anticipation of waking up early to sneak an early peek at the loot under the Christmas tree. My sister and I would try to be quiet but our excitement got the better of us and we would wake our parents from restful slumber so we could begin tearing off wrapping paper and ripping open boxes to discover the hidden contents.

When I became a parent, the roles reversed. After staying up late on Christmas Eve to assemble toys, the last thing I wanted to do was to drag my sleepy head out of bed in the wee hours of morning. I just wanted to snuggle deeper into the covers and ignore my sons, hoping they would just go away for a while so I could sleep.

I remember one Christmas when my sons received remote control cars from Santa. I was roused early that Christmas—around 2 or 3 a.m.—with the sound of cars racing up and down the hallway outside the bedroom door. The boys were trying to be quiet and considerate but the whirring of the little vehicles as they bumped into walls and furniture finally made me realize that I wasn't going to return to a deep sleep that morning. I gave in and got up.

Although I no longer have to rise early on Christmas morning, I love going outside when darkness still envelops the earth like a piece of black velvet sprinkled with glitter. Each time I open my front door and step outside to get my early morning newspaper, I inhale the fresh air and the quiet in anticipation of "the day that the Lord has made."

I cannot remember which days of the year that my morning newspaper is not published—there are very few—so that employees can have the holiday off. Although I miss sitting down to read the news after I read my Bible and my devotional, I miss my reason for going outside that early. It is in the hushed moments of the morning air that I can hear God's voice most clearly. Even when the weather is nippy, I like to linger for a few moments and savor that precious time when all seems right with the world.

Imagine if you will, a silent night in Bethlehem "where the cattle are lowing and a poor baby wakes. But the little Lord Jesus, no crying He makes."

Even though His bed is in the hay, He lies quietly, making no sound. What was He thinking? Was He, too, enjoying His father's company in the early morning?

As you open your Christmas package, in hope of receiving your heart's desire, remember the eternal gift that our heavenly father presented to the world over 2,000 years ago. It is the only gift that brings everlasting satisfaction.

The Gift that Keeps on Giving

"If there is a poor man among your brothers in any of the towns of the land that the Lord your God is giving you, do not be hardhearted or tightfisted toward your poor brother. Rather be openhanded and freely lend him whatever he needs." *Deuteronomy 15:7-8*

Walking out of church on a recent Sunday morning, I was hit by a cold wind that had blown in during the two hours I was indoors. I had not dressed for the abrupt change in weather.

As I fought the strong gale, I clutched my sweater tighter around my shoulders, thankful that I would soon be in my warm vehicle and then, even warmer home. I started my ignition and felt the blast of heat. It was then that I started thinking about the words of the visiting pastor, who had spoken that morning about her mission work in Rio Bravo, Mexico. The picture she painted of the poverty there and the difference that was being made by "gringos," as she laughingly called herself came to mind.

She talked about the ongoing construction of small living quarters for the natives, who were used to living in makeshift homes, some made of nothing but cardboard. She compared the size of their new abodes to a walk-in closet in many American houses.

I thought about my own closet, stuffed with too many items—shoes, purses, slacks, blouses, dresses, jeans and sweaters. Lately, I've been sorting through my clothing and giving away many of those items to people in need. I am guilty of buying too much, usually just because it is on sale.

Recently, when interviewing a local woman who is doing short-term missions in a foreign country, I was reminded again how blessed I am. Lisa, a registered nurse, has made three trips to Nicaragua this past year. Her passion is making a difference and sharing the love of the Lord with these people, most of whom live in squalor in thatched huts with dirt floors. It is one of the poorest countries in the world.

Both women, the visiting pastor and the nurse on a mission, made similar comments about their work. "We go out to make a difference in other's lives and find sometimes, that we have been changed in the process."

During the holiday season, most of us are filled with the generosity of giving, as we are called to do during this time of the year. However, we forget that the needs of the less fortunate don't end with the passing of December. Food pantry shelves still need to be stocked. Homeless shelters still require volunteers to cook and serve meals. Children still need warm clothes. Those without shelter still require a place to call their own, even if it is only a warm place to lay their head at night and a retreat away from a world that can sometimes be cruel.

When we remember that we are blessed by the Lord to be a blessing to others, then celebrating Christmas should become a way of life and not just a season.

When the Tears Come

"You number my wanderings; Put my tears into your bottle; Are they not in your book?" *Psalm 56:8 (NKJV)*

I had my life together—or so I thought. At least I had been telling everyone that I was "just fine" when I was asked.

However, when a co-worker asked me about my Christmas Day, I wasn't prepared for my body's reaction to her question. I dissolved into tears when I realized I had just been going through the motions when we opened gifts and shared a meal at my oldest son's home on December 25.

I, who had always been the strong one for everyone else, could not function that day. I had to leave work.

One life-changing event after another in 2007, including the unexpected death of my father and the more recent loss of a close friend, had finally caught up with me. I had prayed about each one. God had given me the strength to keep putting one foot in front of the other. I kept repeating, "I can do all things through Christ who gives me strength." Philippians 4:13 became my reminder when I wanted to give up.

But I had forgotten one important detail. I had not given myself permission to grieve. I thought tears were a sign of weakness.

Instead, I kept pressing forward, ignoring the fact that I needed time to rest and reflect. I also needed to cry. Tears have come, but often at very inconvenient times, and usually when I least expect them.

Recently, I learned some fascinating facts about human tears. Scientists have discovered three kinds of tears, each with its own distinct quality. Tears released in moments of intense feelings contain more of the protein-based hormones prolactin, adrenocorticotropic hormone and leucine enkephalin (a natural painkiller). These hormones build up to high levels when the body withstands emotional stress. Tears are the body's coping mechanism, whether it is lubricant for our eyes, a cleansing system to remove a foreign object or to release pain and grief. When we ignore the last one, the chemicals associated with stress can weaken the body's immune system. Weeping actually does a body good.

Archaeologists in Israel have uncovered ancient "tear bottles" or wineskins, used to catch and preserve the owner's tears during times of grief or extreme pressure. When David, who wrote Psalm 56, cried out to God, he was under duress. Each time David cried, he asked God to put his tears into His bottle or in this case, a wineskin, count them all, and write them down in His book. He wanted God to remember all of the bad things that had happened to him.

Although I had recognized God as my source of strength, I had not expressed my pain. He understands my grief. He understands my tears, which I tried to deny.

When tears come unexpectedly for what I have lost, I will now let them flow and cleanse my soul. Then, I will ask God to preserve them in His bottle and acknowledge them in His book.

Get off the Pity Pot

"Consider it pure joy, my brothers, whenever you face trials of many kinds." *James 1:2*

I blew my nose, wiped away the snot and decided to get off my pity pot.

I made a vow—life is not going to get me down because I have remembered that God is in all my circumstances.

Although 2007 wasn't the best year I've ever had, I have learned that without tribulation, we cannot grow spiritually. Through trials, we learn to trust God more.

For some reason, last year was a challenge for many people with whom I have visited lately. Maybe it was the ice storm that hit in January or the one in December. Both left thousands in the dark, wondering after several weeks when power would be restored. Maybe it was the uncertainty at the gas pumps as prices rose and fell at the whim of who knows. Maybe it was more personal, like the loss of a loved one, or health problems that were unexpected.

Many of us have spent more time in the valley than on the mountaintop this past year. But life in the valley is where battles are lost or won. Reaching the top is anticlimactic, even if it is more peaceful. How can we appreciate the view from the mountain if we haven't endured the climb?

For Christians, it's not so much a question of whether we'll have to face a trial but a matter of when. We can become discouraged as we struggle up that hill, only to look back and see that we haven't come as far as we had planned. Therein lies the problem—our plans. God has a much better plan for our life than we can even conceive. But if we take our eyes off of Him, it's easy to feel sorry for ourselves and climb back onto our pity pot.

God calls us to be faithful right where we are, even if it is in the valley. If we belong to Him, then we can rest assured that things happen for a purpose. Sometimes, it's only when we look back that we see His perfect plan at work. When I do, I am simply amazed at His goodness.

Faith is a life-long journey, through the valleys and up the mountaintops. It's not a one-time shot after we've come to accept the Lord as our Savior but a daily recommitment, remembering that His mercies are new each morning.

Without struggle, there is no victory. I was reminded of this recently when, in my busyness, I forgot to water one of my favorite exotic plants. When I saw the leaves drooping pitifully, I picked up the pot and set it in my kitchen sink. I left the faucet on to drip slowly into the parched soil, hoping my beautiful plant would survive.

Later that day, revived by moisture, the plant showed no signs of distress. It was a reminder to me that even when we struggle, God will provide all we need to overcome.

Fully Rely on God (F.R.O.G.)

"And so we know and rely on the love God has for us. God is love. Whoever lives in love lives in God, and God in him." 1 *John 4:16*

Sometimes I have trouble falling asleep at night. As I lie in bed, waiting to slip into dreamland, my thoughts drift to problems that I finally realize I cannot change. However, just when I think I have relinquished them to God, I find myself still struggling to let those doubts go.

Several months ago, I found an inexpensive way to help me drift off to sleep. It's a small machine with multiple choices of sounds to soothe and relax, including rain, a waterfall, the ocean, the rain forest, a heartbeat, and my favorite, a summer night.

As a child growing up in Louisiana, I loved warm summer evenings when my sister and I, and other neighbors, would go frog hunting. It was challenging to track them by following the sounds of their voices lifted in harmony. I can still recall using our mother's Mason jars and our father's flashlights to hunt down the creatures who tried to elude us.

Capturing them was easy when our beam of light compelled them to freeze. Getting them in the jar was more difficult if you were squeamish about picking them up. If you could manage to use the jar to scoop them up and slap the metal lid on, you could avoid touching their slimy skin. I didn't mind grabbing the amphibians, even though our mothers had warned us that frogs caused warts.

The outdoors has always been a source of fascination for me. I recall days spent in the lazy sunshine, soaking up God's love for humanity through His beautiful creations. Clouds, trees, flowers, grass, birds, bugs, and yes, even frogs, were a reminder of how much He must really love us. Think of His creation as one big Valentine, signed with love from your Father.

A recent newspaper article reminded me that God still loves to delight us with His creations. Biologists have announced the discovery of a new species of frog. Native to eastern Oklahoma, the Cajun chorus frog is little—about an inch long. What distinguishes this tiny creature from others of its kind is its chirp.

According to one of the biologists who discovered the new species, you can duplicate the sound by running your fingers across a metal comb. When joined by a chorus of others, the chirp of the Cajun frog is deafening.

How easy it would have been for biologists to overlook a one-inch creature. But God, in his infinite wisdom, decided to make this frog different from the rest of His creations. If it weren't for the unique sound of the Cajun chorus frog, scientists might never have discovered it.

When we discover God's uniqueness, and that He truly loves us, warts and all, life begins anew. Even as we struggle with those things that threaten to rob us of our peace, we can rest assured that when we fully rely on God, His light will show us the way.

A Love Letter to God

"Love the Lord your God with all your heart and with all your soul and with all your strength." *Deuteronomy 6:5*

Each morning finds me sitting in an overstuffed chair near a window where I can view the trees in my backyard. Although darkness conceals much of the view, I can still see the branches silhouetted against the early dawn colors. With Bible, devotional and journal in my lap, I spend this time with the Lord. It is the most peaceful part of my day.

In the past, I hit the ground running each morning, fretting about all of the demands on my time. My to-do-list looked like the Pentagon's plan for military intervention in some foreign country. My thoughts and plans were focused on my family's needs, my job and my own selfish desires. I had no idea that God wanted a personal relationship with me.

About seven years ago, events led to major changes in my life. My youngest son left for college. My marriage fell apart and my job no longer provided the satisfaction that it once had. I began to question many things about my life, as well as my purpose.

When Jesus began to tug at my heartstrings, I began to examine my priorities. I also became aware that my greatest need and desire was a relationship with Him.

I know God is not surprised by my thoughts, words or actions. Even though my morning time with Him has become a priority, I still struggle sometimes to be completely authentic with Him. I know, however, that I can hide nothing from Him.

Since I am a wordsmith, I find that writing a letter to God each morning is easier than voicing my fears and my hurts aloud. However, I have to remember that He wants more from me than that. He wants to hear my praise. He wants to know that I love Him for who He is and not just for what He can do for me. When I take the time to give thanks, and to realize how really blessed I am, my writing becomes a love letter to Him.

If you are a parent, imagine how it would feel if your children never expressed their love and appreciation to you. For me, the three most wonderful words I ever hear from my sons and grandchildren are "I love you."

Recently, after much prayer, I made a major decision concerning a job. I felt the Lord's leading even though I struggled with the outcome. Inner peace followed my decision but fears about the future kept resurfacing. I had forgotten that the first commandment is to love Him with all your heart, soul and strength. This also means trusting Him.

Why, then, did I have second thoughts about my decision? Sometimes, in our faith walk, we forget how much He really loves us because it is difficult for us to grasp how wide and long and high and deep is the love of Christ.

It is an unconditional, radical love for His children. Do you feel the same about Him?

Through the Looking Glass

"When I was a child, I talked like a child, I thought like a child, I reasoned like a child. When I became a man, I put childish ways behind me. Now we see but a poor reflection as in a mirror; then we shall see face to face. Now I know in part; then I shall know fully, even as I am fully known. And now these three remain: faith, hope and love. But the greatest of these is love."
1 Corinthians 13:11-13

When I was a child, I struggled with my self-image and my self-esteem. I didn't like what I saw when I looked in the mirror. I was born with naturally curly hair and raised in a humid climate that often created a halo of frizz on my head.

I now realize that my curly hair is a blessing. However, as a teenager growing up in the 60s, I was very sensitive about my wild mane.

My locks earned me the nickname Curly Ann. I hated that name, even if it was bestowed with affection by an uncle. I was very sensitive about my hair.

I coveted sleek, straight tresses that flowed around my head when it was tossed over my shoulder to impress a member of the opposite sex. I wanted hair like Cher and other stars portrayed on the cover of popular magazines.

In the days before hair-straightening tools and salon-style straightening products, girls with curly hair didn't have many options. I remember the first time I convinced my mother to use a chemical straightening product on my hair. Although it tamed my locks for a while, it was only a temporary fix.

Forty years later, I still battle my naturally curly hair. It has a mind of its own. My arsenal of hair care products and equipment rival the Pentagon's store of weapons. However, I've come to accept that it is part of who I am.

God is probably smiling at me as I go to war with my hair each morning. No matter how hard I try to subdue my curls, they eventually return to their natural state; however, my thick, naturally curly hair makes me unique.

Uniqueness is part of God's plan. Before we were born, He chose every detail of our bodies, including our hair. He even knows the very number of hairs on our head.

As my relationship with Him has grown, I have come to realize how much He loves me, just the way I am. I now look in the mirror and see a reflection of His creation instead of an image that society dictates with its multitude of "perfect" models on glamour magazine covers.

When I stepped through the looking glass, I began to acknowledge the person in the mirror. I saw myself through His eyes. What I see is love and acceptance.

Because I did not fit in with the world's definition of beauty, I felt unworthy. As I have come to know my Savior, I now understand that my self-worth is rooted in Him—and there is no greater love.

Innocence in a Pink Tutu

"...The Lord does not look at the things man looks at. Man looks at the outward appearance, but the Lord looks at the heart." *1 Samuel 16:7*

She was innocence in a pink tutu, purple snow boots and a red cowboy hat. You couldn't miss her and I'm glad I didn't.

I still recall the precious child I encountered several years ago while I was shopping in a department store. Who could forget her attire or her smile? She was probably four-years-old, a wonderful age when you are not yet aware of, and really don't care about, others' opinions.

I can only say that I admire the child's mother for allowing her daughter to appear in public dressed so unconventionally. When I was a young mother, I can recall being overly concerned with my sons' choice of clothing as well as my own.

Eventually, I did get past the phobia enough to allow my youngest one to be seen in public in shorts and cowboy boots. He was, however, a pre-schooler. I used that as an excuse to overlook his choices.

My son, now 27, recently showed up in a pair of jeans that had seen better days. We were planning to eat at a local restaurant. When I asked if he had another pair to wear, he became upset with me. He could not understand why I was questioning his choice of clothing. I could not understand why, at his age, he would want to go out in public in jeans that looked like moths had filled up their bellies with enough fabric to last through the winter.

When I had an opportunity last year to interview a veteran, who is also a community volunteer, I learned a lesson that I will never forget. Decked out in black leather, a dew rag and tattoos, he is an intelligent, caring individual. As we talked, the conversation turned to God. He showed me a tattered New Testament that he always carries with him, including to Vietnam. As we visited, I learned that he had once visited a church where someone had looked at his attire and asked him not to return.

I was astonished. If we are to be a reflection of Christ, should we not be like Him and look past the exterior to see the person within?

In 1 Samuel 16:7, God tells the prophet Samuel to go to Bethlehem to anoint one of Jesse's sons as the future king. God warned Samuel not to judge the sons by their looks or height, which might have been easy because Saul was tall and handsome. Instead, God told Samuel, "The Lord looks at a person's thoughts and intentions."

When God told Samuel to select David to succeed Saul, He saw a man after His own heart. We are often tempted to judge people by their looks or their dress, but God can tell what they are. He judges men by their heart.

If we want to emulate Christ, shouldn't we be doing the same?

When I am Weak

Paul wrote, "When I am weak, then I am strong."
2 Corinthians 12:10

Before I retired from teaching three years ago, I religiously kept a daily to-do-list and a monthly calendar that helped me to stay organized. As I finished each task on my list, I would draw a bold line through it. I felt a great sense of accomplishment. I also felt in control of my life.

I also recall others who said, "If you want something done, ask Carol. She can accomplish anything she sets her mind to." I think part of that was because I didn't want to disappoint people. I let their expectations dictate my growing to-do-list.

As my relationship with God has grown, I have struggled with letting go of the need to be in control of my "things to do" and my calendar. While it has brought freedom in some areas of my life, in other ways it has been a challenge for me.

Reading my daily devotional one recent morning, I realized that I am not the only detail-oriented person who has faced this reality when one seeks the Lord's will. Like the author of the devotional, I like order, planning and predictability. I didn't want any unexpected curve balls to knock me off my carefully staged life.

However, as I look back over the past three years, I see God's plan for my life unfolding as I have learned to let go of my compulsion to micro-manage the universe. I now understand that it was all about my need to be in control of every situation. Knowing what to expect in a routine each day, I felt safe. I was strong in my belief that everything would fall into place just as I had planned.

Reporting to work at 8:30 each morning gave my life a framework, a reason to get out of bed. I had to be somewhere because people were counting on me and I had to make a living. Thankfully, I enjoyed my 30 years as a teacher.

However, as I have continued to trust the Lord, He is teaching me not to fear what I perceive as disorder in my life. When I am faced with a multitude of tasks or a puzzling situation, instead of trying to force all of the pieces to fit in my timeline, I am trying to step back from the situation and trust Him.

I have come to realize that God has a better plan than I could ever imagine. Although I would like to know the outcome in each situation, God shows me, step-by-step, that I must lean on Him each day. As I have admitted my weaknesses, He has been able to use them for His purposes.

His goals are far greater than those trivial things on my hand-written list. As I make it a habit to follow in His footsteps, my life is becoming more joy-filled. Who would have thought that life could be so simple?

When I am weak, He is strong.

The Cross around My Neck

"And being found in appearance as a man, he humbled himself and became obedient to death—even death on a cross!" *Philippians 2:8*

As an expression of my faith and as a reminder of what Jesus did for me, I wear a cross around my neck. During times of stress and times of uncertainty, I find myself reaching for that cross. Tracing its outline with my fingers, I find comfort and strength in the shape.

Recently, I commented on a beautiful cross worn by a friend. She replied, "A dear friend gave this to me. I am wearing it each day to remind me to pray for her because she is not well."

Before I started wearing a cross around my neck each day, I had a wardrobe of jewelry so vast I probably could have gone more than a month without repeating an item. Although none of those pieces was very expensive, I thought I needed them to improve my looks.

When I began to crave more of Jesus in my life, my external appearance became less important. I began to give away my jewelry to friends or donate it to charity fundraisers. I also felt led to purchase a few more crosses to wear around my neck. My desire for any other jewelry has faded.

As I have grown in my walk with Him, the cross around my neck has also helped me to connect with others in a new way. Each cross has provided an opportunity for me to share my faith. When God prompts me, I have used each occasion to start a conversation. Oftentimes, it has been in a grocery store checkout line when someone has made a comment about the cross around my neck.

With the Holy Spirit's guidance, I have begun to recognize the hunger in others. I have been there.

When my thirst became greater, there was only one way to quench it—and that is His way. He made me aware of the emptiness that sin had caused in my life but He also led me to the foot of the cross.

As a child growing up in the church, one of my favorite hymns was *The Old Rugged Cross*. I can still recall the words as the song was played on the piano:

On a hill far away stood an old rugged cross,
The emblem of suffering and shame;
And I love that old cross where the dearest
and best
For a world of lost sinners was slain.

Although that song still brings tears to my eyes, I now look at the cross through new eyes. It is about love and hope. Even the disciples, shattered by the crucifixion, were discouraged, until He arose three days later.

The apostle Paul focused on the cross because it is the key to the good news. Christ took the nails for me. He took them for you.

The cross around my neck is a reminder of His sacrifice. Because He bore the weight of the cross, we each can have hope for our own lives.

A Tiny Purple Flower

"I know that my Redeemer lives, and that in the end He will stand upon the earth." *Job 19:25*

It was small and almost hidden by the remnants of dead leaves whose brown color still carpeted the cold ground. But the bright purple flower caught my attention.

It was a sign that a new season was struggling to emerge after a harsh Oklahoma winter. It was also Easter. I smiled when I saw the beauty of the flower's fragile petals because it was a reminder of hope renewed with the resurrection of Christ.

I was hiking that chilly Sunday afternoon with my grandchildren and their parents. The sighting of the flower poking its purple head through the damp earth drew me closer to a time in my life when, like my grandchildren, all was right with the world.

My grandchildren's delight in the beauty of the still brown and gray scenery, interrupted occasionally by patches of early blooming grass, made me pause and inhale the crisp air that cleared my head, still fogged by winter's cobwebs. I couldn't get enough.

As we hiked deeper into the woods and down to a stream, I was transported back to my childhood days, before I was aware that the people you loved could disappoint you and before I understood the deep, abiding love of the One who never would. As a child, I could spend hours alone outdoors. While others formed teams to play ball, I was content to sit or lie silently in the grass. Fascinated by bugs, rocks, flowers and blades of tall grass, I was completely unaware of the passing of time.

That Sunday afternoon, as I climbed the hills and then descended through the valleys with my loved ones, time stood still again. Sounds of civilization were overshadowed by the creek water as it tumbled over rocks and bounced off the banks. The occasional sound of a bird punctuated the air, reminding us that we were not alone.

We skipped rocks in the creek that had recently overflowed its banks after a rainstorm had flooded parts of the area. We studied the intricacies of unusual tree roots that had forced their way above ground, yet had withstood the weathering of time and nature. Fascinated by green moss growing on rocks and tree stumps, we touched the velvet fabric with the tips of our fingers.

My larger, time-weathered hand found comfort in holding the smaller hands of my grandchildren as we walked that day. There was no reason to hurry as we stopped to observe other mysteries, like mushrooms and that tiny flower of hope.

Hope, renewed in something as small as a flower poking its head through the brown soil of life and as basic as God's love for us, is His promise of better things to come. It came wrapped in a simple hike through His creation to experience the true blessings of Easter, not wrapped in brightly colored foil or synthetic grass but presented unpretentiously in a magnificent way.

Do You Know Him?

"Know therefore that the Lord your God is God; he is the faithful God, keeping his covenant of love to a thousand generations of those who love him and keep his commands." *Deuteronomy 7:9*

I was recently interviewed for a magazine article because I am a cancer survivor. This June will mark six years since I heard those dreaded words, "You have cancer."

As I answered the questions posed by the woman who was writing my story, I also reflected on God's role in my life. When the interview was over, I was once again reminded of His faithfulness, even during times of my faithlessness.

Although I attended church faithfully through my teen years, I drifted away until my sons were born. Eventually, I returned because I knew they needed a foundation for their own spiritual growth. However, I strayed from my own foundations several times over the following 20 years.

When I found myself alone after my 28-year marriage ended, I was lost because I had never sought a personal relationship with my Savior. One afternoon, as I sat near the lake where I lived at the time, I prayed aloud for the very first time. My prayer was simple, but voiced in despair: "Lord, I need some direction in my life. Please show me the way."

After uttering this simple prayer, I was flooded with peace and the knowledge that life was worth living, especially if I began living it for Him. My life hasn't necessarily been easier since that day, but knowing that He is always faithful has lightened my load.

In retrospect, I see God's fingerprints all over my life. I was not taken to church by faith-filled parents or grandparents. But God planned that my parents would purchase their first new home in a neighborhood that was within walking distance of a small church. It was that same church where I received the foundations of faith that would eventually lead me to trust Him.

As I look back, I know without a doubt that it was part of God's plans for me to survive numerous childhood illnesses and seven surgeries—some very serious—over the next 53 years. His grace has allowed me to thrive and overcome other life-changing events. God has been faithful even when I wasn't.

Recently, I was startled by a conversation with someone whom I have known since my childhood. I have been praying for this person because I love her very much. Like me, she was raised to be an independent woman.

As we discussed our backgrounds, she said, "I know that God has given me talents and that I have accomplished a lot in my life. But He's too busy to worry about me. He has bigger concerns in this world."

I smiled and then disagreed. I don't think that God ever worries and I know that He loves us because we are His children. More importantly, He wants a personal relationship with us.

I have learned, however, that we have to seek Him if we want to know Him.

Do you know Him?

Maker of All Things, Including Mud

"Through him all things were made; without him nothing was made that has been made." *John 1:3*

"In the beginning, God created the heavens and the earth." Even for those who are not Bible scholars, the first verse in the first chapter of the Old Testament is familiar.

God also created mud. As I was walking at a local park during a recent warm spring day, I saw two children playing by the lake. My first reaction when I saw what they were doing was, "Oh, my gosh! I'd hate to wash their clothes." The pair, a boy and a girl around nine-years-old, was having a mud fight.

My second reaction, when I saw their joy was, "That looks like fun." That insight came from knowing the Lord and experiencing His creations, even mud.

As a child, I also enjoyed God's creations. My sister and I loved making mud pies after a spring rainfall. When we were finished, our mother usually hosed us down outside before we were allowed in the house.

As an adult, I am saddened when I see the thoughtlessness of people who carelessly throw their trash along the roadside and in other public places. Although God gave humankind the capability of inventing new products, like plastic and aluminum, they often end up on the ground where they are a threat to the wildlife and the environment.

I was amazed, yet troubled, by a fact sheet that I received with my utility bill. In the informative pamphlet, I learned the following about the litter that dots our landscape and threatens to destroy God's beautiful creation. It takes 10-20 years for plastic bags to biodegrade while aluminum cans last as long as 100 years.

Other statistics were even more disheartening. Here are a list of products scattered about as litter and the years required for disintegration: Styrofoam cups, 1-100 years; tin cans, 50-100 years; plastic 6-pack holder rings, 450 years; glass bottles, one million years; plastic bottles, forever.

A previous neighborhood in which I lived had an over abundance of foot traffic because people cut through on their way to a local store. It was frustrating because careless shoppers' trash littered the streets and yards. I started taking a sack with me on my daily walks to retrieve the waste.

Scripture teaches that the earth belongs to God. "The earth is the Lord's, and everything in it, the world, and all who live in it..." (Psalm 24:1) It is not ours to do with as we please. In Genesis 2:15, one of God's first commandments to Adam says we are to "take care of" creation.

Humankind, however, has not listened very well to the Maker of Heaven and Earth. We have an obligation to protect and restore the gift of God's beloved creation; however, we have to take action to better honor Him and show that we are good stewards of all that He has given us.

Life is God's gift to you. The way you live it is your gift to God. How are you living your life?

One Medium Suitcase

"For we are God's fellow workers; you are God's field, God's building." *1 Corinthians 3:9*

When my pastor said, "One medium suitcase," I replied, "Define medium."

He was speaking at a planning session for our Rio Bravo trip. It was my first international mission trip and I was excited. However, I needed to know the exact parameters for packing. We would be driving to Mexico on our church bus. Nineteen team members would be giving up eight days of their time—some even taking vacation days—to make the 1,900 mile round trip. Space on the 25-seat vehicle also had to be reserved for our luggage and necessary supplies for some of the mission projects.

We were also packing VBS materials and housewarming gifts for the family who would be the recipient of our main project. In four days, we planned to construct a 12 x 20 casita from concrete blocks, wood and tin. The small building, with two doors, three windows and a loft, would house a family of five when completed.

The young couple, with three daughters from one year to seven, had been living in an adjacent dwelling almost half that size. The casita, when finished, would not have plumbing or electricity.

Our Mexican partners in mission had already prepared the foundation for the new home. Like others on our volunteer team, I found myself laying concrete blocks the first day. I was hesitant at first. What if I couldn't do it? What if I messed up? I had never done this kind of work before.

After observing the others at work, I realized that I could do it too, and if I messed up, I could scrape off the layer of cement and start over. I grabbed a trowel and began adding mortar to a concrete block. The walls grew taller as we worked side-by-side to create the house that would become a mansion for this family.

As the four walls began to take shape, the smile on the young mother's face radiated excitement. Although most of us spoke little Spanish, verbal communication was not needed. Facial expressions revealed her thoughts and feelings. Her anticipation was contagious and the children soon warmed to our presence.

With basic tools, we were able to construct the casita in three and one-half days. When completed, it did not house a leather couch or designer drapes. But in the midst of poverty, I saw wealth through the eyes of the grateful couple that would move their meager possessions into the new dwelling.

When I recall my pastor's instructions about a single medium suitcase, I picture the young family and realize that much of what I packed in my luggage was not a necessity. Although I thought I could not do without some of those items, I came to appreciate the fact that less is better.

For in the giving of ourselves, we became God's fellow workers. In traveling to a foreign country, we were His field and as we erected the larger shelter, we became His building.

Love in Any Language

"By this all men will know that you are my disciples, if you love one another." *John 13:35*

As our mission team traveled on the bus to Rio Bravo, Mexico last month, those of us with limited Spanish vocabulary studied hand made flash cards. We needed the basics, especially the word "baño" for bathroom.

By the time our 895-mile journey ended just across the border, we felt ready to communicate, at least for the week we would be there. Although we understood more than just informal greetings like "hola!" for hello and "adiós," for good-bye, our vocabulary was limited when trying to convey a more complicated message. We found ourselves using hand gestures and Americanized versions of the language to communicate with the residents of the community.

One day, during a break from our labors, three of us were craving ice cream in the 97-degree weather. We entered a small store next door to the work site. One of our team members tried unsuccessfully to ask the proprietor if he carried the frozen treat. Using my hands to express our request, I began to mimic the licking of an ice cream bar. The storeowner smiled and brought forth a candy sucker. Shaking my head from side to side, I then clasped my hands around my upper arms as if to indicate I was cold. I shivered and said, "Brrrrrr."

He smiled and went to the back of his grocery where he opened a freezer for our inspection. He waved us around the counter where we were allowed to select our own treat. It was exciting to make ourselves understood, even without words.

I saw this action repeated again during the week as we helped conduct a three-day Vacation Bible School for area children. Even though we had two interpreters on our team, the number of children present each day prevented us from relying fully on their services. We had to depend on our own resources and limited Spanish vocabulary to communicate with the children, who ranged in age from one year to approximately 12.

Bible lessons were presented in Spanish to the group of excited boys and girls in the small hot church where we had classes. However, when the children divided into small groups for crafts and activities, we faced another communication gap.

Their laughter, as well as ours, as we tried to make ourselves understood, put smiles on everyone's faces. As the youngsters became accustomed to our ways, we felt loved by their hugs and touched by the kisses on our cheeks. Each set of big brown eyes revealed a hunger for understanding.

Steven R. Covey, a leadership consultant, had this to say about compassion: "The more deeply you understand other people, the more you will appreciate them, the more reverent you will feel about them. To touch the soul of another human being is to walk on holy ground."

When walking in love or "el amor," we are following the commandment of Jesus whose love knew no borders. Do you speak His language?

A Mother's Legacy of Love

"Listen, my son, to your father's instruction and do not forsake your mother's teaching." *Proverbs 1:8*

Until my mother passed away almost four years ago, I sometimes struggled to find the right card to express my sentiments on Mother's Day. I struggled with choosing a card with a nostalgic poem or one with a humorous slant. Maybe it was because my mother always seemed so much in control of her emotions.

I don't recall my mother's tears. I do remember her frustrations, especially at the end of her life when her body, crippled with arthritis, began to fail.

Unlike my gregarious father, my mother didn't share many of her childhood memories. However, I do recall a story she told us the Christmas before she died.

Like my father, my mother grew up during the Depression when economic conditions led to hard times for everyone. As we ate our Christmas dinner, we discussed those days when families were forced by circumstances to be resourceful.

My father, the storyteller, related tales of his mother's ingenuity during those hard times. She took in boarders and laundry. She baked and sold pies and took in sewing. Because there were six mouths to feed, she scrambled to help her husband put food on the table.

My mother's mother grew a garden and raised chickens. My mother related a story to us that Christmas about occasionally being allowed to take an egg to a local general store to trade for a candy bar, a treat during those years. She was careful as she walked the mile to the store, afraid that she might trip and break her precious commodity.

It was this story that touched me. I could imagine my 78-year-old mother as a young girl. She was probably barefoot and wore a homemade cotton dress, handcrafted with love by her mother. In my mind, I pictured her cradling the egg in her hands and slowly walking a dusty road to exchange it for a candy bar.

My heart then ached for my mother whose health no longer allowed her the luxury of even doing her own grocery shopping. She relied on my father or one of her two daughters to make the purchases, including an occasional candy bar.

After my mother died in July 2004, my sister and I talked about those things that she had taught us. More than a homemaker who cooked from scratch and made all of her daughter's clothes, she taught us responsibility.

Each Saturday morning, we would find a list of chores posted on the refrigerator door. Before going out to play, we had to complete our assignments. She also taught us the skills of organization as well as being responsible for our belongings. She instilled in us a work ethic that remains today.

My mother also modeled compassion. Whether it was home baked food or clothing or a kind word, she reached out to others in need.

As Jesus taught His disciples, my mother instilled in her daughters a legacy that only love can buy.

Bringing Home the Birkin

"Command those who are rich in this present world not to be arrogant nor to put their hope in wealth, which is so uncertain, but to put their hope in God, who richly provides us with everything for our enjoyment." *1 Timothy 6:17*

Rarely do I watch television. If I sit still that long, I fall asleep. I occasionally flip through the channels while I am doing something else, like housework or putting on my makeup in the morning. Usually, I listen to one of my favorite pastors or watch the home and garden channel.

Sometimes, a news program captures my attention. That was the case on a recent weekday when I heard a news commentator talking about bringing home a Birkin. Of course, I had to stay tuned for the rest of the story after the commercial break. I had never heard the term. Was it a new automobile? Had someone come up with a new invention that would revolutionize housecleaning? Or had someone come up with a new designer dog, like my Chiweenie Taco?

I was more than amazed when I learned that a Birkin is a woman's handbag. What is more astounding is the price of the handbag, ranging in price from $8,500 to $200,000.

For more than 20 years, the Birkin bag has been a symbol of fashion, luxury, and wealth with a fabled waiting list of more than two years to purchase one from Hermès. According to news accounts, it is the "most coveted" handbag of the rich and famous.

I have to admit that I love purses. I have too many in my closet and they are all black. Why black? Because it is a basic color and goes with anything. However, my purses, usually purchased at one of our local stores, easily cost less than a tank of gas for my Honda Passport.

That's why my jaw dropped when I heard the price range quoted for a Birkin. Wow, what I couldn't do with that amount of money. Like helping others who can barely afford to buy a tank of gas to get to a minimum wage job.

Although it has been more than a month since our mission team returned from Rio Bravo, photos of our trip remind us that there is still much to be done in this world. One of my fellow team members, reflecting on our mission, said the following: "There were lessons learned. The biggest lesson was how little we really need to be happy. There was so much love among our group and between our group and the people. Rio Bravo was not just a mission to the people of Rio Bravo. We were also in mission to each other. Rio Bravo has had a lasting impact on my life. My goal is not to forget the lessons learned there."

The most important lesson to remember is to put our hope in God, who richly provides us with everything for our enjoyment. We really don't need much to be happy. Who needs a Birken?

Quit Your Bellyachin'

"Do everything without complaining or arguing, so that you may become blameless and pure, children of God without fault in a crooked and depraved generation, in which you shine like stars in the universe." *Philippians 2:14-15*

We're all guilty. We've griped about slow traffic or that crazy driver who pulled out in front of us. We've complained about our boss, the weather and the high price of gasoline.

A recent ABC new story captured my attention because a Kansas City, MO. pastor had decided to do something about whining, which he believes has become a national epidemic and a roadblock to better things in our lives. Pastor Will Bowen says, "I wanted people to stop focusing on what they didn't have in their lives and complaining about it, and to start focusing on what they do have in their lives and being grateful for it."

Bowen came up with a plan. He handed out purple rubber bracelets to his congregation with instructions to move them from one wrist to the other each time they uttered a complaint. His goal was for each person to go 21 days without moving the bracelet. "I believe that your mind is a manufacturer, and your mouth is a customer," says Bowen. "And if the customer stops buying what the manufacturer is producing—in other words, you stop complaining, the manufacturer retools, and you literally start thinking happier thoughts."

Bowen admits that it took him three months to go 21 consecutive days and he broke three bracelets in the process just switching it back and forth from one wrist to the other. Eventually, he stopped griping.

According to news reports, so did members of his congregation. According to one church member, going "complaint-free" has changed their lives in a number of ways. "I feel happy. I feel reborn, like a kid again."

Since starting their campaign, the church has shipped out 5.3 million bracelets worldwide to people who want to quit complaining. Bowen's goal is to distribute 60 million of the purple reminders worldwide.

Even God's chosen, the Israelites, who were led out of slavery in Egypt by Moses, were whiners. God orchestrated their escape from bondage through a variety of events, including the ten plagues and the parting of the Red Sea. God provided everything they needed for their journey but because of their frequent complaining and failure to trust Him, God made them stay in the desert for forty years before they reached the Promised Land.

After my mission trip to Mexico last month, I realize I should have nothing about which to complain. When I recall the smiles on the faces of those who live in houses that are smaller than my double car garage, I am humbled by God's goodness and inspired by the warm welcome we received from the natives there. They live simple lives of gratefulness.

Can you imagine what our world would be like if everyone quit bellyachin' and started counting their blessings? We could all use a purple bracelet as a reminder.

How Great a Father's Love

"Look at how great a love the Father has given us, that we should be called God's children. And we are!" *1 John 3:1 (HCSB)*

I was cleaning my office when I came across the birthday card my father had given me before his passing last year. When I opened the card and read the words, the tears started flowing. Then, when I reread the first line, penned by a Hallmark writer, I was astonished.

"Although I've known you since before you were born, somehow, you still amaze me."

Before I was born? Those words had not registered with me when I read the card on my birthday in 2006. Now, I contemplated them and recalled Jeremiah 1:5: "Before I formed you in the womb I knew you, before you were born I set you apart..."

After perusing God's words in Jeremiah, I read the next line of my card. "I've watched you go through change after change. And I've seen you navigate through some pretty rough times with your heart as your compass and your strong, resilient spirit to carry you through."

It was as if the writer of the card had peeked into my life and seen the hurdles I had faced and eventually overcome, including divorce, cancer, my mother's death, retirement, moving to a new community and starting over. Without my heavenly Father, I could not have made it through these trials. Through His guidance and strength, I grew stronger and more confident that whatever happened, He would be there.

Before my father's brief illness and death last September, I also had confidence that if I needed him, he was only a phone call away. Although his job took him away for weeks when I was growing up, he was available to help when I needed him, even after I had children of my own.

A conversation with an older friend recently reminded me of the influence our fathers have in forming their children's lives. One day, my friend allowed a playmate to paint her fingernails a bright red. "I was so proud of my nails," she said. "I couldn't stop looking at them."

My friend continued admiring her nails until her father drove up the driveway from work. She was so excited to see him that she promptly forgot about her nails. She jumped on the running board of his automobile—as she did each day. Her bright red nails were on display as she clung to the side of the window frame.

"Upon reaching the house, he asked to see my hands," she said. "I couldn't hide them from him, or the fact that I had done something of which he disapproved. I was so ashamed because I had disappointed my father. I never wanted to do that again."

Like my friend, I never wanted to let my father down. It was one of my greatest fears when I was a young girl.

I also never want to disappoint my Heavenly Father whose love is so great that he calls me his child.

Called to Be an Overcomer

"They will fight against you but will not overcome you, for I am with you and will rescue you,' declares the Lord." *Jeremiah 1:19*

Whenever I am able, I love to spend time with my grandchildren. Yesterday was one of those days.

After I receive kisses and hugs, both my granddaughter and my grandson have to show me their latest "ouwees." You won't find that in Webster's dictionary but I came up with my own spelling based on their pronunciation and the sound of "ouch." Although I don't know where they came up with this term, I understand its meaning. It is any place on their body where they have a scratch, bump, bruise or pain.

My granddaughter's latest tale concerning a bruised fingernail was revealed in detail. My grandson, however, can tell his story in fewer words, even if he has a prolific vocabulary for someone who is getting ready to turn three.

I've had my own share of "ouwees," and they didn't end when I outgrew childhood. My latest, in 2007, required a two-day hospital stay and 17 staples in my right calf.

When we suffer physical wounds, we usually turn to medical science to help us recover. With my grandchildren, a kiss to the small wound is usually enough to satisfy their immediate pain. At other times, we have to look in the medicine cabinet for a salve, spray or a band-aid. Sometimes, we have to go to a doctor.

Listening to a conversation between two pastors on television this morning reminded me that we all experience our share of both physical and spiritual wounds, no matter what our age. As they discussed wounds, I began to take notes, as I often do, because I am interested in growing spiritually.

A wounded spirit, when trust is breached, was one of the four spiritual wounds the two discussed. One pastor is the author of the book, "Healing the Wounded Spirit." He revealed a struggle he had gone through when he was betrayed by a friend. Following that, a series of events that he began to dwell on, led to depression.

That period of depression made him immune to his own beliefs and preaching about faith. Even his well-meaning, positive friends aggravated him with their homilies until he said he finally turned to the Lord. I was amazed at that revelation. How often do we preach but don't follow our own advice?

I've experienced my share of spiritual depressions when I've tried to solve the problem by covering it up. I've ignored the signs and forgotten to trust the One who can help me heal. Sometimes we're too busy bleeding to look for answers.

When we realize that our God is the Great Physician, then we can turn to Him for healing in any form, but especially for spiritual healing. Like a cast takes the load off a broken bone until it heals, our Lord takes our burdens and slowly our spirit begins to heal.

We are called to be overcomers, but God doesn't expect us to do it alone.

Sustained by Promise, Living in Hope

"Sustain me according to your promise, and I will live; do not let my hopes be dashed." *Psalm 119:116*

I was on my cell phone as I drove by a local gas station. When I saw the price, $4.99, I exclaimed to my listener, "You're not going to believe the price of gas here."

I did the math and realized that the amount was a whopping $1.20 difference from the previous day. "That can't be right," I said.

Down the road, I saw the price was still $3.79 at another store. Although I only needed an eighth of a tank, I pulled in and topped off my tank to the tune of $13.79. When I bought my Honda Passport in 2001, I could fill up for $15.

When my cell phone rang, I told a friend about the price jump. Neither one of us could believe it. She said, "That has to be a mistake." So, I turned around and drove back to the station where I had seen the big bold numbers announcing the increase. I knew I had not been dreaming, but when I arrived, the price was $3.79.

It is easy to become discouraged or angry when we fill up our gas tanks. Turn on the daily newscast and listen to the predictions and it can dash your hopes of relief anytime soon. I have tried to understand why gas prices are soaring. I have read the newspaper and listened to news commentaries as well as friends' rantings—and yes, I have complained too. But to no avail.

I don't even pretend anymore to understand, or try to understand, the complicated workings of mankind. As I was filling my tank recently, a man at the next pump said, "If prices keep rising, I'll be forced to sell a kidney to pay for gas."

Of course, I laughed, but then I wondered why he was driving a gas-hogging automobile. I didn't ask, but I had to pray for God to keep a guard over my tongue. Otherwise, I would have found myself preaching to him.

It is easy to preach to others when we think we know best. It is even easier to make assumptions about the things of this world and find ourselves hopeless when we feel it is out of control. I have had to learn the hard way that my attitude and reactions are the only things I can master—and I don't always do a good job.

Almost four years ago, when my mother's serious illness forced us to move her into a nursing home, I felt helpless. So did my mother. She had to depend on others for even the simplest of tasks. One day, as I helped her to the restroom, she said, "Carol, I never thought it would turn out like this."

While we might not be prepared for the way things turn out on earth, I know that my Savior came to offer hope. He has promised to sustain us and we can have peace knowing that He always provides for our needs.

Freedom to Choose

"It is for freedom that Christ has set us free. Stand firm, then, and do not let yourselves be burdened again by a yoke of slavery." *Galatians 5:1*

For more years than I care to count, I was a slave. No one held me captive behind bars. Loss of freedom was my own choice.

However, I was in my late 40s before I realized that I could be free. I allowed the opinions of others, and my own desire to please others, to hold me hostage. When I disappointed others, I felt guilty and inadequate.

Most people were unaware of my insecurities. People who didn't know me very well thought I had my life together. I did on the outside. I worked hard at putting on a mask of perfection.

I became an overachiever, seeking accomplishments and accolades to bolster my self-esteem. After reaching the top of the ladder in my profession, I felt nothing except emptiness.

Despite my achievements, I felt incomplete and often wished that I were someone else. I thought that if I performed well or appeared attractive on the outside, it would carry over into my internal life. I didn't know that I could only find inner peace that comes from knowing who you really are in Christ.

After my Savior set me free, I came to realize that the real meaning in life is not the product of what you have or don't have, or what you've done or haven't done. Because I am a child of God, I am already a whole person with a life of meaning and purpose.

As my relationship with Him has grown, so has my freedom to make choices. In the past, when I was asked to take on a task, I would not only do it, but also excel at it. Often, my decision to accept the offer was based on flattery that I had been chosen to do the job. I thought I had to continue to prove myself.

God loves us so much that He gave us the freedom to make choices. Although some are of little consequence, others are life-changing. We have all made poor choices. However, there is good news because no matter our past, there is always hope for a better future.

Recently, I overheard a conversation at a local store. An elderly woman was in a handicapped cart, while a younger woman, whom I presumed to be her daughter, was juggling children, an overflowing grocery cart and a calculator.

As one of the children begged his mother for a toy, she was going through the cart taking an inventory of its contents. When the child continued to plead, she snapped at him. The older woman reproached her and the mother replied, "I have no choice. I've never had a choice."

I didn't know her history but my heart went out to her because we do have choices and the most important choice we can ever make is to choose freedom through a relationship with the Lord.

Have you made that choice?

Some Things Never Change

"I the Lord do not change. So you, O descendants of Jacob, are not destroyed." *Malachi 3:6*

As I was shopping recently, I overheard someone say, "Some things never change." I didn't hear the rest of the conversation but I had to agree.

Fights between siblings never do change. My grandson, trying to elicit sympathy from me during a phone conversation, said, "Nana, Cheyenne won't share her toys."

"What did you do?" I asked him. He replied, "I hit her."

I just had to chuckle because some things never do change.

As a friend and I discussed this topic, we concluded that the following things do not change: there will always be wars because people will disagree; all people will eventually die, the sun will always rise in the east and set in the west; people will complain about the weather, whether it is hot or cold, wet or dry; no one can change the past; no one can accurately predict the future; no one can change another person; there will always be poor people who need help and there will always be people who take advantage of others; there are always people who genuinely want to make a difference in this world and there will always be people who think only of themselves.

My list could go on. However we view the world in its constant state of change, some things never change. Even with technological advances, humankind never really changes. If you go back to the beginning of the Bible and follow man's attempt at making things work on his own, you can see that some things never change.

In the beginning, when God created the heavens and earth, and then Adam and Eve, He had only one rule: "You may freely eat any fruit in the garden except fruit from the tree of the knowledge of good and evil. If you eat of its fruit, you will surely die."

Of course, we know what happened next. Eve was tempted by Satan to taste the fruit, which she shared with her husband. When God discovered what they had done, He confronted Adam. What did he do? He blamed his wife. Humankind is still playing the blame game today. Some things never change.

We know the story of 99-year-old Abraham, and his wife, Sarah, who had a son, promised by God nearly a decade and a half earlier. Before that, the impatient couple took matters into their own hands and Abraham produced a son by his wife's servant, Hagar. Some things never change.

Peter got out of the boat and walked on the water toward Jesus. But when he saw the wind, he was afraid. He began to sink. Crying out, he said, "Lord, save me!" How often do we take our eyes off the Lord and start sinking in fear? Some things never change.

Human behavior never changes. We can be grateful, however, that the One who created us also never changes. Even when everything around us may be changing, His steadfast love will save us from ourselves.

Too Good to Be True

"We know also that the Son of God has come and has given us understanding, so that we may know him who is true. And we are in him who is true—even in his Son Jesus Christ. He is the true God and eternal life." *1 John 5:20*

When my father was alive, he had a unique way of getting rid of telemarketers. When the voice on the phone started its spiel, Dad would reply, "You know I have something to sell too. I have about 80 head of Black Angus cattle. How many would you like to buy?"

Usually the telemarketer would sputter and then hang up. Dad would start griping about having his supper interrupted. While I can sympathize with someone who is trying to make a living, I also become annoyed when a salesperson telephones with big promises. Although I have signed up for the Do Not Call list, my phone occasionally rings and my caller ID reveals an unknown number. If I don't answer, a mechanized voice on my answering machine tries to entice me to return the call so they can save me money on insurance or some other product or service.

While I am not opposed to saving money, I have learned the hard way that if it sounds too good to be true, it probably is. I have, however, fallen prey to those seductive infomercials that promise quick results with the latest gadget to help you get in shape in 30 days or less or your money back. I can recall exercise equipment and tapes that I have purchased in the past and usually returned because they did not live up to the promised benefits. Although my money was refunded, I had to pay for postage and a restocking fee. If I am fortunate, I receive at least 75 percent of what I spent in the first place.

If you have ever received an offer that just sounds too good to be true, I know you can relate. However, it's not just junk mail, telephone calls and television advertising that have lured us to part with our hard-earned dollars. The Internet has become another tool to bombard us with offers of quick riches, fast weight loss, quack health products and other quick bullets to solve all of our problems.

Recently, a news program revealed several of the latest frauds that prey on consumers' desire to get better gas mileage. Who wouldn't want to save on gas by purchasing an inexpensive contraption? However, as the newsperson demonstrated the products, he revealed the reason each would not work based on scientific evidence. Still, some people had parted with their money, taking a chance that it would prove to be the answer to rising gas prices.

Why do we fall for man's promises that are too good to be true yet hesitate to believe the only truth that we can really count on as revealed in God's word? Through His Son, we can count on eternal life. That's the best guarantee we can ever receive.

Praise the Lord

"I will tell of the kindnesses of the Lord, the deeds for which he is to be praised, according to all the Lord has done for us—yes, the many good things he has done for the house of Israel, according to his compassion and many kindnesses." *Isaiah 63:7*

My three-year-old grandson recently asked to pray before a meal. My son or his wife usually offer the blessing before eating but this time Brennan volunteered.

Brennan bowed his head, folded his tiny hands in prayer, squeezed both of his eyes tightly shut and then remained silent for a few moments. Then one eye popped open and he glanced around the table and began to pray. "Thank you Jesus for the food. Thank you for the milk. Thank you for the fork. Thank you for my sippy cup. Thank you for my chair..."

However, Brennan didn't stop there as he continued to look around the room and offer thanks for everything he could see, including his toys and his parents. The prayer, according to my son, was more than five minutes long as he instructed his parents and his sister to repeat each line after him. The food grew cold as Brennan continued his praise.

I can remember a time in my life when my prayers were learned by rote. You know the kind I am talking about; the ones that we learned when we were merely children in Sunday school. "God is great and God is good and we thank him for this food. By his hand must all be fed; Give us, Lord, our daily bread. Amen."

One prayer that I remember well hung on my bedroom wall when I was a child. Inscribed on a ceramic plaque were the following words: "Now I lay me down to sleep. I pray the Lord my soul to keep; if I die before I wake, I pray the Lord my soul to take. Amen."

When my first grandchild was born, I gave the keepsake to my son with instructions to keep it in the family. When my daughter-in-law decorated Cheyenne's room, she hung the prayer by the crib.

Recently, I was cleaning bookshelves and organizing my home office when I discovered one of my prayer journals. For more than 10 years, I have kept a daily prayer journal. I had overlooked this earlier one when I decided to keep all in a safe place for my eyes only. As I thumbed through and reread some of the dated entries, I felt the peace of God settle around me. The ink-filled pages, some tear-stained, were a wonderful reminder of God's faithfulness. Even though some of my pleas had gone unanswered, I felt renewed hope when I saw how my faith-walk had grown.

My love letters to God are now filled with praise for what He has already given me. I ask for less but receive more. He has already given me more than I deserve and more than I could ever imagine.

When we seek to praise, our prayers reflect his compassion and kindness. Have you praised God lately?

Are You a Worrywart?

"Therefore do not worry about tomorrow, for tomorrow will worry about itself. Each day has enough trouble of its own." *Matthew 6:34*

"If worry were an effective weight-loss program, women would be invisible." When I read this quote recently, I had to laugh because it's the truth. Does that mean women worry more than men do?

Regardless of your gender, almost everyone worries about something whether it is finances, health, work, or family issues. However, if you worry 24/7, you just might be a worrywart.

According to dictionary.com, a worrywart is a person who tends to worry habitually and often needlessly. Recent studies indicate that 85 percent of all that we worry about never happens. These include worries over our past, which we can never change, worries over which we have no control, irrational concerns or fears and future worries.

Over 100 diseases have been directly attributed to worry. The strength of your immune system is related to many factors, including worry. Worry not only robs you of your physical energy, it can steal your peace of mind. Worry can raise your blood pressure, harden your arteries, and put wrinkles on your face and dark circles under your eyes.

Worry will not make your problems go away, help you deal with your problems, or make you feel better. It only robs you of today's joy.

We can easily become discouraged by daily headlines of doom and gloom. But can we change those things? I like this anonymous quote: "Worry is like a rocking chair; it keeps you busy, but it doesn't get you anywhere."

So what is the answer to worry? If you believe scripture, then the only answer is prayer. When we are facing difficulties, we should focus on God and not the problem because He has our best interests at heart. We should also focus on His resources and what He has promised us in scripture; third, we should not focus on the obstruction but look at it as an opportunity for God to demonstrate His love.

I recall reading a devotional titled "God's Bag." The writer instructed readers to write their worries down and place them in a brown paper bag. Following the instructions was this letter:

My dear child,

Today I will be handling all your problems. Please remember that I do not need your help. Write your worries down and kindly place them in the God bag. It will be addressed in my time, not yours. Once the matter is placed into the bag, do NOT hold on to it or remove it. Holding on will delay the resolution of your problem. If it is a situation you think you can handle, please consult me in prayer first. Because I do not sleep, there is no need for you to lose sleep. Rest my child. If you need to contact me, I am only a prayer away.

Love,

Your Heavenly Father

Because the Lord our God is with us always, we need not worry about tomorrow.

It Is Well with My Soul

"Dear friend, I pray that you may enjoy good health and that all may go well with you, even as your soul is getting along well." *3 John 1:2*

Four funerals were held recently in one week at our church. I was able to attend only one. Of the four hymns chosen by the family, one resonated with me. As I left the church that day, I found myself singing the words.

Because the song stuck with me, I wanted to know more about its origin, so I googled the title, "It is Well with My Soul." In 1873, a prominent lawyer Horatio G. Spafford wrote the lyrics after three major traumas in his life. The first was the loss of his only son in 1870 to scarlet fever. A year later, the Great Chicago Fire ruined him financially. Shortly afterwards, Spafford lost all four of his daughters in a ship collision while crossing the Atlantic. His wife survived and sent a telegram: "Saved Alone."

Anna Spafford was saved from the fate of her daughters by a ship plank, which floated beneath her unconscious body and propped her up. After Anna's rescue, her first reaction was one of complete despair. After hearing a voice speak to her, "You were spared for a purpose," she recalled the words of a friend, "It's easy to be grateful and good when you have so much, but take care that you are not a fair-weather friend to God."

After Spafford heard the terrible news, he boarded the next ship out of New York to join his grieving wife. During the voyage, the captain of the ship called Spafford to the ship's bridge to point out where he believed the other ship had gone down. According to history, Spafford returned to his cabin and penned the words of the hymn that come from 2 Kings 4:26. His words reflect the response of the Shunammite woman to the sudden death of her only child. Although scripture tells us "her soul is vexed within her," she still maintains, "It is well." Spafford's song also reveals a man who has put his trust in the Lord in spite of the tragedies.

A friend and I were discussing the words to this song. She said that someone once told her that instead of greeting someone with, "How are you?" we should ask, "How's your soul?" When asked the first question, we usually reply, "Fine, thank you," or "Okay." Our response does not require much thought, even if things are not going well in our life.

However, when we ask someone "How's your soul?" that person has to think before replying. Some people never complain but they may be in pain—physically, emotionally or spiritually. When we ask this question, we reveal our heart, and like Horatio Spafford, we gain strength in the knowledge that our Heavenly Father works all things for good to them that love Him.

No matter what circumstances we face in life, may we be able to say, "All is well with my soul."

When God Blesses Your Socks Off

"O Lord Almighty, blessed is the man who trusts in you." *Psalm 84:12*

As I was driving across town recently, I began to praise God for all of the many blessings in my life: my family and friends, my church family, my health, my finances, my beautiful home, my dog, and my vehicle. My 2001 Honda Passport is just about broken in as I am nearing 100,000 miles. I thanked the Lord that my reliable automobile had been running smoothly.

Things changed in the next 30 minutes when I left an office building and tried to start my vehicle. The battery was dead. After calling a friend to give me a jump with his battery cables, I told him about my praises to God. I said, "God does have a sense of humor, doesn't he?"

My friend laughed and said, "Yes, because after I told you I would help you, I realized I was in my son's car and I didn't know until I got here whether or not he had any jumper cables in the trunk." Thankfully, there were two and we only needed one to get my car back on the road.

When I arrived home and pulled my vehicle in the garage, I turned the engine off. I then attempted to restart my car to see what would happen. I'm glad I did because the battery was dead again. Later that evening, my son arrived to help me push the vehicle outside to charge it again. Nothing happened. As we drove to an auto parts store to get a new battery, my son said, "Mom, it might not be the battery. It could be an electrical problem."

I knew that an electrical problem would be expensive—definitely more expensive than a new battery. I started praying, "God, please let it be the battery. Please let it be the battery."

As the store employee tested my battery, I continued to pray. When he announced that the battery was 100 percent dead, I said, "Thank you Jesus!" I just didn't realize, until the man looked at me quizzically, that I had said it aloud. I told him: "I'd rather fork over $100 for a new battery than be faced with an expensive repair bill on the electrical system."

Before I placed my trust in the Lord, I would have been worried about the money I had to fork over for a new battery. Thankfully, I could afford the $100, plus tax, and I'm sure that if the alternative was an expensive repair bill, God would have provided. He always does.

I have a girlfriend who has been through a nasty divorce, the loss of a dear friend, and a serious car accident that left her with physical and mental challenges. However, she never complains. She is always upbeat because she knows that God provides for her needs and more.

As my friend says, "God always just blesses my socks off."

Although I have never heard that expression before, I have to agree with my friend. Now where are my socks?

Does It Really Matter?

"But blessed is the man who trusts in the Lord, whose confidence is in him. He will be like a tree planted by the water that sends out its roots by the stream. It does not fear when heat comes; its leaves are always green. It has no worries in a year of drought and never fails to bear fruit." *Jeremiah 17:7-8*

About 50 percent of Americans, according to statistics I have read, live within 50 miles of their birthplace. This phenomenon is known as propinquity. I belong to the other one-half of the population who do not live within that vicinity.

Born in Lake Charles, Louisiana to parents who were native Oklahomans, I relocated to the northeastern part of this state in 1969 with my family. During the past 39 years, I have only returned to the state of my birth twice. The most recent was in the summer of 2002 when my sister and I made a road trip to visit friends and our old neighborhood. While there, we stopped by the elementary school we had attended. Peering through the classroom windows, we were nostalgic as we speculated about the spot where we had sat over 30 years ago.

On a recent weekend trip to another northeastern Oklahoma town where I had previously lived, I stayed overnight with a friend in my old neighborhood. Josie, who is known for her hospitality, also welcomed my dog, Taco. Although I had only returned for a few brief visits during the three years since I had moved, Taco had not forgotten where my friend keeps her own dog's feeding dish.

Taco also remembered the house across the street from Josie as the first home he had known with me. While we walked the tree-lined streets of this peaceful neighborhood, he pulled on the leash, trying to redirect my attention to the wooden steps that lead to the house at 1319 Wood Street. The house that overlooks the lake is full of memories made during the four years that I lived there after my divorce and where I finally found inner peace through a relationship with my Lord.

During our visit, Josie, who is a native of Spain, shared memories of the first 25 years of her life. Although my 79-year-old friend has only returned to visit her birth country a few times since moving to the United States, she knows her roots are now planted on Wood Street in Grove, Oklahoma.

When I felt led by God to move to Claremore, many of my friends had a hard time understanding my move and questioned my choice. However, I didn't.

Although I still miss my lake house, as well as my friends, like Josie, if you look closer at the meaning of the word, propinquity, you just might understand more about our awesome God. Synonyms include affinity, closeness, connection, nearness, proximity, relationship and togetherness.

No matter where we were born or where we have planted our roots, God is always with us. It is His closeness and our relationship with Him that really matters.

Who Is Really in Control?

"Those who live according to the sinful nature have their minds set on what that nature desires; but those who live in accordance with the Spirit have their minds set on what the Spirit desires. The mind of sinful man is death, but the mind controlled by the Spirit is life and peace; the sinful mind is hostile to God. It does not submit to God's law, nor can it do so." *Romans 8:5-7*

For more months than I care to count, presidential candidates have been touting their solutions to America's problems. As usual, there is much mudslinging, name-calling and finger pointing. This year's campaign has brought more attention than those in the past for several reasons. No one wants to accept responsibility for the mess in which our country currently finds itself and politicians think they have all the answers. People are asking, "Who is in control?"

I, like many Americans, have become disgusted with politics as usual. I sometimes find myself choosing the lesser of two evils when I cast my vote at the polling booth. Many people with whom I have talked feel the same.

Candidates make promises they cannot keep because they want to win or they truly feel they have the power to change the status quo. Some people want to believe these promises because they are looking for hope. However, they are placing their faith in man and not God.

Recently, I received the following via email:

Top 10 Predictions (No Matter Who Wins the Election)

1. The Bible will still have all the answers.
2. Prayer will still work.
3. The Holy Spirit will still move.
4. God will still inhabit the praises of His people.
5. There will still be God-anointed preaching.
6. There will still be singing of praise to God.
7. God will still pour out blessings upon His people.
8. There will still be room at the Cross.
9. Jesus will still love you.
10. Jesus will still save the lost.

Seven years ago this month, I was searching for direction in my life. I was mourning the end of my 28-year marriage. Marriage counseling had not helped. I had placed my faith in man's counsel. I was lost until I turned to the One who is really in control.

My simple words on that sunny October afternoon were voiced aloud in prayer. "God, I need some direction in my life. Please show me the way."

God has not only shown me the way but He has given me the strength and courage to stay on the chosen path. While many are wringing their hands and voicing their doubts about the direction that our country is headed, those of us who trust in our Lord have reassurance that no matter who wins the election, God is still in control. We live in a country with many blessings, including the opportunity to choose our leaders.

His name may not be on the election ballot but isn't it great to know who is still in control?

I'm Doing It for Jesus

"Whatever you do, work at it with all your heart, as working for the Lord, not for men..." *Colossians 3:23*

"I'm doing this for Jesus." I had to keep saying those words as I cleaned up the mess I had made when I removed a pizza from the oven. The heat from the oven had fogged my glasses and I didn't realize that my lunch was slipping from the pan until it was too late.

The pizza landed face down on the baking racks. It's like dropping a slice of bread slathered with peanut butter. For some unknown reason, it always ends up face down on the floor. When I saw the cheese oozing through the openings to land on the electric coils, I sighed. Not only was my lunch on the bottom of the oven, I still had to clean up the gooey debris.

My oldest son called while I scraped the cooled remnants of my lunch off the delicate inner workings of my oven. Of course, he had to laugh about my mishap. "Next time," he said, "take your glasses off before you open the oven door."

"That's a great idea," I said, "but without my glasses I probably couldn't find the pizza without sticking my head in the oven to locate it."

As I talked to my son, I had more insight into the mess I had made. I told him, "I really don't like cleaning up my own disasters but I don't mind cleaning the mishaps of others."

"Why is that?" he asked.

"I don't know," I replied, and I didn't at the time. As I reflected on my reply, I realized that when I do things for others I feel blessed to be a blessing.

When my son and his wife lived in Texas, I would often drive down to visit. The house they were renting did not have a dishwasher. Since they both worked long hours at the time, I used the opportunity to clean their house, including washing and drying the dishes. I enjoyed the chance to do something for my loved ones.

This year I started volunteering one afternoon a week at our church's front door ministry. For four hours, I am able to assist those who have come seeking help with their utility bills or in need of groceries for their families. Often, I am overwhelmed by the stories I hear from those who are barely able to make ends meet. Since the economy has worsened this year, our ministry has grown from serving about 700 per month to over 1,200.

I look forward to serving each Tuesday afternoon because I realize that I am doing this for Jesus. In Matthew 25:40, Jesus tells His disciples, "The King will reply, 'I tell you the truth, whatever you did for one of the least of these brothers of mine, you did for me.'"

As I fill bags of groceries each Tuesday afternoon, I am reminded that we must all celebrate our blessings, even if it means cleaning pizza off the oven racks.

The Gift of Yourself

"How much better to get wisdom than gold, to choose understanding rather than silver!" *Proverbs 16:16*

I love old people. Now, define old. The main entry at dictionary.com says the term, an adjective, means advanced in age. If you're in your teens or twenties, old might look like a 40-something. If you're in your thirties or forties, old might look something like a 50-year-old plus some years. You get the idea.

I like the synonyms for the word, "old." Words like experienced, mature, seasoned, skilled and veteran are listed in the dictionary as words that mean the same or almost the same. Other meanings include constant, enduring, established, familiar, long-lasting, solid and steady. I like these: sagacious, sensible, and venerable.

Recently, I was reading a story about a 97-year-old woman, who started a new career four years ago. At four feet ten inches tall and with snow-white hair, Mae Laborde is now a Hollywood actress. At 93, she took her first casting call, which led to a commercial, followed by other television appearances. She's also been a cheerleader on ESPN and is now in a movie with Ben Stiller.

When a reporter asked Mae about the secret of living a long life, she replied, "Never retire." At eighty-nine, she took a police training course, just for fun. She cooks for herself, loves to paint, raises a garden, and sells her produce to a local restaurant. Now that's what I call spunk.

I recently had the pleasure of teaching two seasoned veterans in my writing class. Both have many lessons to share from their years of experience. Their delightful attitude about growing older is a gift to anyone who wants to receive what they have to offer.

Hazel, who just turned 80, is working on her family's memoirs so that her six children and 10 grandchildren will have a family history. Hazel, however, is in no hurry to complete the project because, as she says, "I plan to live to be 120, so I have plenty of time."

Ruth, whose resume includes nurse and nurse anesthetist, returned to college later to earn a MBA. At the age of 73, she earned a PHD in criminal justice. As she nears 80, she continues to take classes for enrichment and growth. She is also currently working toward her goal of writing 225 poems, which will be published in the near future by a company who has requested her work.

During the seven weeks that these two wise women attended my class, they continually amazed and amused me with their spirited attitudes toward living life to the fullest. Hazel called me on the last day of class to tell me that she wasn't feeling well and would not be able to attend because, as she said, "She had been burning the candle at both ends."

Wisdom and understanding comes with age, but sharing what one has learned with others is truly a gift. You can't store up treasures on earth, but you can enjoy them while they are here if you understand the value of what others have to offer.

Don't Give God Your Leftovers

"If there is a poor man among your brothers in any of the towns of the land that the Lord your God is giving you, do not be hardhearted or tightfisted toward your poor brother." Deuteronomy 15:7

I never saw his face. However, with his back toward me, I could see the slumped shoulders as he ate the warm meal that had been provided by our church. A woman had discovered him sleeping in a local park and dropped him off at the front door of our church.

He was temporarily homeless by choice. Circumstances forced him to leave the apartment he was sharing with another. He had nowhere to go. Phone calls failed to turn up a suitable place for him to stay. Funds from our Good Sam ministry, and that of another area church, paid for two nights at a local motel. He is currently staying with one of our church members until permanent assistance can be found for him.

Recently, a friend related a story about another homeless man who was living in a tent behind the business where she works. After visiting with him, she and other employees began to provide help, including a warm blanket. When his tent accidentally caught on fire, he escaped, carrying only the blanket provided by someone who cared. However, the story doesn't end there. The employees have purchased new clothing for him and made phone calls to find the medical attention he needs.

Neither of these homeless men's stories is finished and neither is God's call on our lives to help others. During a recent sermon on generosity, our pastor reminded us that God doesn't want our leftovers. He wants our first fruits. Generous giving enables us to care for others.

What would the world be like if each of us took it upon ourselves to reach out to another human who is in need without expectation of return? Instead of providing our leftovers to the poor, what if we gave them our best? Isn't that what God did for us? He gave us His best in the form of a small child named Jesus.

All good things come from God, including His grace. It doesn't matter if you call it *grace, gratia, charis,* gracia, grazia, gunst, or any other language, the meaning is basically the same. Grace is "a showing of kindness, a favor done without expectation of return, an act of mercy."

At some point in our lives, we have all experienced grace. Someone has shown us kindness. Without expecting anything in return, someone has done us a favor. As humans, we have a capacity for grace. No human, however, can come close to expressing the grace that God has shown us. Nothing can compare to His Amazing Grace.

The ultimate witness we can present to the world is the love we have for one another. That love flows from the very heart of God.

The holiday season is upon us. Let us prepare our hearts for giving.

The Gift of a Memory

"Above all, love each other deeply, because love covers over a multitude of sins." *1 Peter 4:8*

When I try to recall store-bought gifts I have received, I cannot pinpoint any one present I unwrapped that has special meaning for me today. However, I can recall the memories that have come with unique gifts that money cannot buy.

A recent birthday gift from my sister has special meaning and brought back memories. First, the gift came from the heart, and second, it is a reminder of my maternal grandmother and her gifts. The gift, an African violet, now rests on my kitchen table where I can see it each time I sit down to eat. What makes this gift so special?

When my grandmother passed away in 1973, my mother kept some of the prized plants for which she was known. I can remember the beautiful plants that lined my grandmother's windowsill and decorated other areas of her house.

The plant that my sister gave to me last month has been propagated from one of my grandmother's original African violets. For over 30 years, my mother, and now, my sister, has kept my grandmother's legacy alive through this beautiful plant.

Another special birthday gift came unexpectedly from a new friend. Although the coffee mug was not a family heirloom, it brought tears to my eyes as I realized its significance. First, the giver of the gift had parted with a piece of her own history, an object that had belonged to her grandmother. Second, the simple white mug was a carbon copy of one that my own father preferred to use when he drank his morning coffee.

After my father passed away last year, my sister and I sorted through his household belongings. I didn't keep many of my father's things. I am trying to simplify my life by not hanging onto material possessions. However, when I saw the heavy white mug in its simplicity, I knew without a doubt that it was given in love. It now has a place of honor on my kitchen cabinet where I can see it each time I fill one of my own mugs with hot tea. It is not only a reminder of my father but of the giver of the gift.

With the kick-off of the holiday season, I was once again reminded of how crazy our world has become. Recent headlines about Black Friday grabbed my attention. Although I am not against saving money when shopping, the lengths to which people go to purchase a gift for a loved one always amaze me. Horrified, I read the story about a store employee trampled to death by out-of-control shoppers, eager to get a bargain at 5 a.m. What was more chilling was the fact that the bargain hunters kept on shopping after the store manager announced the store would close because of the incident.

I pray that others who don't understand the true meaning of the greatest gift in the world will turn to the One who gave us the greatest gift of all, His Son.

Unwrap Your Christmas Gift

"But the angel said to them, 'Do not be afraid. I bring you good news of great joy that will be for all the people. Today in the town of David a Savior has been born to you; he is Christ the Lord. This will be a sign to you: You will find a baby wrapped in cloths and lying in a manger.'" Luke 2:10-12

With hard times affecting everyone, there may not be as many presents under anyone's tree. Wouldn't this be a good time to recall why we celebrate Christmas in the first place before commercialism seized this holiday and turned it into a three-ring circus?

Wouldn't this also be the perfect time to quit racking up credit card debt and a time to consider what we already have and be thankful, instead of eyeing someone else's treasures with green-eyed envy?

I am still disturbed by the death of a Wal-Mart worker who was killed when an unruly crowd trampled him in their eagerness to get bargains on Black Friday. What is happening in our world? How did it get so out-of-control? What motivates people to get up before dawn to save a few bucks on gifts that will end up forgotten by the next Christmas when the cycle starts all over?

I found the following suggestions for "Ten Gifts that Don't Cost a Penny" by Martha Lash that we all might consider in light of what is happening now:

1. **The gift of listening.** Listen without interrupting or daydreaming.
2. **The gift of a compliment.** A simple and sincere compliment can make someone's day.

3. **The gift of a favor.** Perform a kindness each day without expecting anything in return.

4. **The gift of a cheerful disposition.** An easy way to feel good is to speak kindly to someone, even a stranger. You'll also make their day.

5. **The gift of a written note.** A brief handwritten note, not an email, may be remembered and treasured for a lifetime.

6. **The gift of solitude.** Be sensitive to the times that others need time alone. Respect their wishes and give them their space.

7. **The gift of saying "Thanks."** Make a conscious effort to say, "Thank You," every time someone does something for you. Soon it will become a habit, bringing happy   feelings   to everyone.

8. **The gift of laughter.** I've always said that a man who can make me laugh is worth his weight in gold. Help people laugh. It's good for their health— and yours.

9. **The gift of affection.** Express your affection appropriately with a pat on the back, a hug or holding hands to demonstrate your love for family and friends.

10. **The gift of prayer.** There is no greater gift you can give another than praying for them. Be sure and let them know that they are on your prayer list.

However, the greatest Christmas gift we will ever unwrap is the one given to each of us by our Father over 2,000 years ago when our Savior was born And, it is the only gift with eternal significance.

The Story Is Not Over

"For God did not send his Son into the world to condemn the world, but to save the world through him." *John 3:17*

As I was studying and reflecting on my Advent devotions, I thought about those who don't have Christ in their lives. Maybe they have never heard the Good News; maybe they have chosen to reject the news because they think it is just too good to be true or maybe, they don't believe the story is for them.

Sometimes, I find it hard to believe that someone living in America with its proliferation of communication methods might not have heard the greatest story every told. In a bruised and broken world, the positive news is easily overshadowed by news of greed, war, famine, genocide and the economy.

Then, I wonder about those who are unbelievers. Why have they made that choice? Maybe the rational human mind cannot comprehend a love so great that God would send His only Son into the world to save us.

What if Mary had chosen not to believe the angel, Gabriel, who appeared with the news that she would give birth to a special son? Even in her uncertainty, she chose, in her childlike faith, to commit herself to God's plan.

As small children, we live in hope, expectantly waiting and watching. With wide-eyed wonder, we look at the opportunities presented to us. However, somewhere along the way, life happens and we forget that "Nothing is impossible with God."

As we grow up and gain confidence in our own abilities, we forget to give credit where it is due, to the One who knew us before we were ever born.

Arrogantly, we march forth on our own journey and ignore the signs all around us. Even when confronted with evidence, we claim to be masters of our own universe.

Consider, however, the results of a recent survey, asking respondents if they believed in miracles. Of 1,300 people 45 and over, fully 80 percent said they believe in them. Eighty-four percent of those who believe attributed miracles to God. About three quarters further identified Jesus and the Holy Spirit as sources of modern-day miracles.

Albert Einstein, a German-American physicist, once said, "There are only two ways to live your life. One is as though nothing is a miracle. The other is as though everything is a miracle."

Patsy Clairmont, a Christian speaker and author, says, "I think that through miracles we step back and we start reevaluating our place in the universe. We see something miraculous and ask ourselves, 'What is this? I can't explain it. Is there truly something more than me?'"

It's when we say "Yes" to God that the real miracle begins. With our consent, He performs a life-saving heart transplant and we are never the same. With our transformation, we begin to see life through His eyes. It's only then that we realize the story is not over if we allow God to illuminate the darkness through our lives.

Life Is Like a Roll of Toilet Paper

"I press on toward the goal to win the prize for which God has called me heavenward in Christ Jesus."
Philippians 3:14

If Mr. Whipple were still alive and doing Charmin bathroom tissue commercials, I'm sure he would agree with Andy Rooney's observation that life is like a roll of toilet paper. The closer it gets to the end, the faster it goes.

With that statement, I would ask, "Where did 2008 go, and are you prepared for the New Year?" When we hear the words "new year," most of us start making resolutions to improve ourselves in the coming year. Considering that the top ten resolutions each year are similar, why do we often fail?

We start determined that this year we are going to do it. However, as the days pass and the calendar changes from January to February and then March, our determination waivers and we soon lose motivation to reach those goals.

Well-known author and speaker, Zig Ziglar, says, "People often say that motivation doesn't last. Well, neither does bathing; that's why we recommend it daily."

Starting each day by reading the Word of God is motivation for me to do what I need to do that day, even if I don't feel like it. That doesn't mean I get everything accomplished, but without encouragement from scripture and devotions, there are some days that I would probably give in to despair.

I recently attended the funeral of a 28-year-old man who died in an automobile accident. I didn't know him, but his aunt is my best friend. My heart ached for his family, especially for the seven-year-old son he left behind. As I listened to my friend speak about her nephew during the service, I learned that even in his short life J.J. had lived each day to the fullest.

In the book, "One Month to Live: Thirty Days to a No-Regrets Life", authors Kerry and Chris Shook ask the question: "If you knew that you had one month to live, how would you live differently?"

What would be the focus of your days? Would your priorities change or would you continue to live life as if nothing were different?

As an experiment, the authors challenged their staff members to answer those questions by living the next 30 days as if they were their last and to write down what happened. According to the authors, the results were "nothing less than life-changing," with the group having a greater clarity of purpose and a renewed passion for the things in life that really matter. Some people in the group did big, once-in-a-lifetime things, while others found meaning in their lives by viewing those things they once considered a chore as sacred times that could not be recaptured, like spending more time with their children or their aging parents.

What if we lived each day as if it were our last? Following in the footsteps of the apostle Paul, what if we kept pressing forward, staying focused on the Lord so we could hear those words, "Well done thy good and faithful servant?"

What Is Your Story?

"The man who saw it has given testimony, and his testimony is true. He knows that he tells the truth, and he testifies so that you also may believe."
John 19:35

I believe everyone has a story to tell. So does StoryCorps, a project launched in 2003, who uses this premise to interview everyday Americans by permanently recording details of personal anecdotes and experiences. Through a permanent recording booth in New York's Grand Central Station and mobile units traveling around the nation, citizens can create 40-minute recordings to capture poignant and inspirational stories that are archived with the American Folklife Center at the Library of Congress.

As of January 12, 2008, over 10,000 interviews have been recorded, and the numbers continue to grow. With all of the celebrity interviews and news we are exposed to daily, we might think that ordinary people like us have nothing to share. However, we have all experienced personal triumphs, losses, and other situations that make compelling stories.

As I have grown in my walk with the Lord and learned to listen to the stories of other Christians who are on the same journey, I have been inspired by those who have been there before me. Their struggles, their joys, their humanness makes me realize that following Christ does not make us exempt from trouble and pain. But it is also exciting to share our faith walk with each other as a source of encouragement, especially when we are struggling.

I was reminded of this when I recently read the story of a local man who will be the first recipient of a prestigious mentoring award in Oklahoma. I interviewed Mr. Parker several years ago for a newspaper article I was writing on volunteers in our county. Mr. Parker shared his testimony with me, including surviving stage-three esophageal cancer. He said, "God had a reason for leaving me here for awhile longer."

Parker's second chance at life has turned into opportunities to help others, including being a mentor to youngsters, becoming a leader of Bikers Against Child Abuse (BACA), serving as a hospice volunteer and finding time to visit with hospitalized veterans. His story needs to be shared so others might be inspired to give back.

Christian author and speaker, Elisabeth Elliot, says, "It is God to whom and with whom we travel, and while He is the God of our journey, He is also at the stopping places."

It is at those stopping places where we must share our stories of faith with others. I like to call them my "God Stories."

John the Baptist was a prophet whose own coming was prophesied by the prophet Isaiah over 700 years before as the voice of one crying in the wilderness, telling people to get ready for the coming of Jesus. John told his followers "He is the one who comes after me, the thongs of whose sandals I am not worthy to untie."

John's purpose was to prepare the people to accept Jesus. How can your story help others to accept Jesus?

Making Do with Less

"I know what it's like not to have what I need. I also know what it's like to have more than I need. I have learned the secret of being content no matter what happens. I am content whether I am well fed or hungry. I am content whether I have more than enough or not enough." *Philippians 4:12*

In the current economic crisis, many are looking for ways to solve their financial problems. A recent CNN news story captured my attention because a family was selling most of their belongings, including their children's toys, to pay off debt.

When I heard this story, I thought about my grandchildren who have too many toys. Several weeks ago, my daughter-in-law was tired of trying to get them to pick up their toys. After several warnings, she finally picked up and bagged every toy by herself. She placed every toy the two possess in the garage for a week. During the time Cheyenne and Brennan were without a single toy, coloring book, crayon or stuffed animal, they entertained themselves by playing with empty laundry baskets and boxes, amusing themselves with their indoor pets, wrestling with each other and dancing to music. My daughter-in-law reports that the two fought less during that week and they didn't nag her to give their toys back.

As each bag of toys has been returned to my grandchildren, the two have been instructed to keep them in their proper place or the toys will go to a charity. So far, it looks like the charity is going to reap the benefits of my grandchildren's disobedience.

In today's society, most of us are consumed by the desire for more. We are also a wasteful society. When we are not content, we constantly search for that elusive "object" that will make us happy but can lead to serious debt.

As a friend and I discussed this topic over lunch recently, she shared stories of her family life when she was growing up in northeastern Oklahoma. I was amazed when she told me that she had not experienced the luxury of indoor plumbing until she went to college in the early 70s. Her family did not own a telephone or have an indoor restroom until after that time. While most of us take indoor plumbing and a telephone for granted, we might be surprised to learn that there are some in this country who cannot afford either.

Another recent discussion about our society's wastefulness provided this insight. The person with whom I was talking mentioned his mother-in-law's habit of hanging on to scraps of aluminum foil to reuse because she had grown up during the Depression years. We both agreed that many of us today could not survive the tough times that our grandparents and great-grandparents did because we are too wasteful.

We need to use this current crisis in our country to learn to be content, whether we have more than enough, or not enough. It is up to us to make do with less and help others who really do have less.

Inside the Empty Nest

"Therefore I tell you, do not worry about your life, what you will eat or drink; or about your body, what you will wear. Is not life more important than food, and the body more important than clothes? Look at the birds of the air; they do not sow or reap or store away in barns, and yet your heavenly Father feeds them. Are you not much more valuable than they?"
Matthew 6:25-26

On a recent unusually warm February day, I took advantage of the weather to go for an outdoor walk instead of spending time at the gym. I would rather be outdoors anytime, even in the winter. It is where I find peace when my days have been hectic. I also know that I will see evidence of God's presence, even in the browns and grays of the landscape.

I wasn't disappointed that day. The bare branches of a tree revealed a bird's nest within reach of my 5'3" height. Although the nest was now exposed to the elements, the leaves of the tree had once concealed its hiding place. I peered inside, knowing it would be empty. However, I was fascinated as I studied the intricately woven haven constructed by one of God's creatures. I wasn't sure what bird species had built the nest, nor did I know how many eggs had been laid in the refuge, but I wondered if all had survived after hatching.

I studied the nest closely. Can you imagine constructing your home without hands or tools? Yet, God designed birds with the ability to fend for themselves. Just as birds know how to fly, they know how to build a nest. Each spring, a natural instinct leads each species to engineer a nest to protect eggs and nestlings from predators and adverse weather.

They instinctively fashion nests that are inaccessible, hidden or camouflaged.

According to "Holman Bible Dictionary," the Bible contains approximately 300 references to birds in both the Old and the New Testaments. In Exodus 19:4, the eagle is used figuratively of God's protection and care: "You yourselves have seen what I did to Egypt, and how I carried you on eagles' wings and brought you to myself." Then, in Deuteronomy 32:11, scripture says, "like an eagle that stirs up its nest and hovers over its young, that spreads its wings to catch them and carries them on its pinions." These passages depict a loving God who redeems and protects His people even as the parent eagle cares for its young.

As worries increase with each day's bad news about the economy, it is easy to forget that we have a loving parent in our Heavenly Father who considers us more valuable than the birds of the air. Jesus encourages us not to worry about that which we cannot control. When God is firmly established at the center of our focus, worry loses its grip on our lives.

If you can recall God's past provision, then you know He cares about His children. When you need encouragement just look at the birds of the air.

Is Your Tongue "Holey?"

"Set a guard over my mouth, O Lord; keep watch over the door of my lips." *Psalm 141:3*

A friend and I were recently discussing the different times in our lives when we wished we had just kept our mouths shut. We've all been there, saying the wrong thing at the wrong moment. Some of us have even earned a t-shirt for "foot-in-mouth" disease.

After we had a lively talk about some of these embarrassing and hurtful moments, my friend told me about a pastor's wife she knew who had trouble keeping her mouth shut. I found the story amusing because the wife revealed she had "a holey tongue."

My friend explained that since this woman knew she had trouble holding her tongue or refraining from speaking her mind, she had resorted to biting it to keep from saying things she should not. Therefore, she had come up with the expression, "holey tongue."

I like this woman's attitude because I have had to learn, the hard way, to keep my mouth shut when I thought I had all of the answers. Like David, I have to ask God continually to keep a guard over my mouth.

Author Robert Newton Peck once said, "Never miss a chance to keep your mouth shut."

Following that advice is not always easy, especially when someone has made an unkind remark or passed judgment. It takes self-control and learning to use the opportunity to grow within yourself when you would rather strike back. I haven't always been successful either.

Psalm 52:4 describes the tongue as a "sharpened razor." If you have ever been cut with a sharp razor or knife, you know the results. If the cut is deep enough, you bleed. The same thing happens when your words hurt someone's feelings. Once you say something, you can't take it back. You can apologize and ask for forgiveness, but the words still hang in the air and color the relationship.

I remember the old rhyme, "Sticks and stones will break my bones but words will never hurt me." I can also recall shouting those words when I was a child and involved with others in a neighborhood spat. The truth is words do hurt, not physically, but emotionally.

In Proverbs 12:18, wise King Solomon wrote, "Reckless words pierce like a sword, but the tongue of the wise brings healing."

I am glad that God's mercies are new each morning because I have been reckless with my words in the past. I don't want to be remembered for those times when my tongue got the best of me. Instead, I want my words to be ones that encourage and lift people up.

As followers of Christ, we are a work-in-progress. He is not finished with us yet. Therefore, I will keep trying with His help to harness my tongue and follow James' advice in 1:19 "to be quick to listen, slow to speak and slow to anger."

I also plan to follow the advice of the pastor's wife and develop a "holey" tongue.

We Are God's Garden

"With my great power and outstretched arm I made the earth and its people and the animals that are on it, and I give it to anyone I please." *Jeremiah 27:5*

Spring, with its smell of freshness and message of hope, is my favorite time of year. With the first hint of warm weather, I start going through seed and bulb catalogs and visiting local nurseries where I browse and plan. I check my garden tools and other accessories to make sure they are ready to go when I know it is safe to start planting.

I don't worry about manicures because I know that when I start squeezing the fresh soil between my fingers, it is the best cure for what ails me. It is getting back to the basics that fill me with peace.

Some of my fondest memories date back to the days when I watched, as well as helped, my grandmothers work in their gardens. Both always wore dresses, even to garden. My maternal grandmother also wore a bonnet to protect her face and neck from the hot Oklahoma sun. I still have one of the flowery bonnets that she sewed from scrap material.

I can also recall running through waving fields of corn in a neighbor's patch in Louisiana where my dad leased land from that same landowner. I grew up in the era of school segregation. The landowner's daughters were not allowed to attend our "all-white" school. However, that didn't stop my sister and I from spending time with the two girls, running through the rows of corn and playing hide-and-seek among the tall vegetation. We were nearly always barefooted. The feel of the cool, fresh earth between our toes drew us closer to our roots and to each other.

When I am on my knees working in my flowerbeds, I feel connected to His greater power. It is like a spiritual retreat as I also use that time to think, pray and meditate on God's goodness. My problems seem miniscule compared to the awesome feeling I get when my hands dig into the brown earth.

Vigen Guroian, a theology and ethics teacher at Loyola College in Baltimore, Maryland, says, "God gives us these growing things as signs and symbols of the redeeming love for the whole of creation. The garden is a place where we can taste paradise."

Guroian suggests that we see ourselves as God's garden. "Thanks to the divine miracle of grace, we can open our petals and shine with beauty."

Lately, I have been doing much soul searching. My conversations with God have not only included my thanksgiving for His blessings, but also asking His forgiveness for my transgressions. I'm glad His mercies are new each morning.

Just as winter has slowly released its hold on the earth, spring has arrived with a new beginning. When we ask for forgiveness, He releases our sins and allows us to begin again. Like the spring flowers that are blooming, God helps us to work toward becoming the persons whom He created us to be.

Have You Been Pruned?

"He cuts off every branch in me that bears no fruit, while every branch that does bear fruit he prunes so that it will be even more fruitful." John 15:2

"If it flowers before June, do not prune." I came across this rhyming advice about pruning after I received conflicting information from two neighbors who also love getting their hands dirty in God's earth.

According to my Internet resource, it is best to prune immediately after flowering. Otherwise, if you prune a spring-flowering shrub in winter or early spring, you cut off all the flowering stems, which have put on growth during the previous year. However, if the plant flowers later in the year, late summer or early autumn, it is safe to prune in late winter or early spring as new growth starts.

This information can be confusing to someone who is a gardening newbie. Trying to learn all there is to know about planting, growing and maintaining flowers, shrubs and trees can give one a case of gardening indigestion.

As I have learned more about taking care of my garden, I have also discovered that there are different implements for a variety of jobs. While I don't have all the tools as prescribed by professionals, I do have a few basics, including shears and loppers.

As I was pruning some shrubs I had planted last year, I discovered something underneath the dead foliage. New growth was poking its head through the soil. I was delighted because I was not familiar with the growth pattern of this plant. At first, I thought it had not survived the winter. I was prepared to pull it from the soil and purchase something else.

I had never pruned my plants, at least correctly, until I became friends with a woman who moved to my neighborhood last year. Dee has a beautiful yard. Her flowers, shrubs and trees are the envy of people like me who would have to use dye to achieve green thumbs. Secretly, I think Dee stays up at night and talks to her plants.

I didn't understand the need for pruning until I did some research after talking to my friend who likes her yard to be neat and tidy. Of course, shrubs and plants have to be kept a manageable size so they don't take over the yard. However, there are other reasons for pruning like cutting out dead or diseased wood from trees and shrubs. Cutting back branches that have become tangled or crossed over prevents damage and promotes new and strong growth.

Just like trees, shrubs and other plants need pruning, so do we. As branches, believers either bear fruit and are pruned to bear more fruit or do not bear fruit and are thrown away.

In order to bear fruit, we must abide in Christ. But even fruitful branches need pruning. Sometimes, just like an overgrown shrub, He has to take away those things in our life that are not productive so we can flourish and continue to grow.

My Savior Lives

"The Lord lives! Praise be to my Rock! Exalted be God, the Rock, my Savior!" *2 Samuel 22:47*

Yellow daffodils and tulips of every hue were trying to poke their heads through the heavy snowfall we had late last month. By the calendar, we marked it as spring. However, Mother Nature had her way and dumped about six inches of snow in our area. Other counties in the state received up to 25 inches, according to weather reports.

One woman, quoted in an area newspaper, said "It's too late. It's springtime. We need more flowers, not snow."

The day after the storm, the sunshine melted the snow quickly, leaving a mess behind. I took my dog for a walk that afternoon and found it hard to believe that just the day before I had watched out my window as the snow had fallen unrestrained, piling up quickly against the side of my house.

Flowers that survived the onslaught were once again seeking the warmth of the sun. I was amazed at how resilient they are.

As I walked through my neighborhood that day, I thought of the previous day's storm. There are times when my life is like that snowstorm, with problems falling relentlessly until I am smothered by their weight. Sometimes, it takes awhile for me to dig my way out. Other times, the sunshine appears immediately to melt away the sadness and like those flowers, my hope springs eternal because I know my Savior lives.

If you had asked me seven years ago for proof that my Savior lives today, I doubt I could have come up with any evidence. Now, as I look back through the years, I can share testimony of His fingerprints all over my life. He has been with me from the beginning. I just didn't realize it at the time.

I knew there was a God. I believed in Him. I believed that His son, Jesus, died on the cross and rose again three days later. However, I didn't understand that He wanted a personal relationship with me. How, I thought, could He care about someone like me?

In late 2001, emptiness filled my being. Nothing could fill that God-shaped hole. Shopping sprees, voracious novel reading and various relationships could not help me escape the void inside my heart. One sunny October afternoon, I pleaded, "God, I need some direction in my life. Please show me the way."

Like the snow melting off the landscape, I felt my heaviness lift. I was no longer lost. Since that day, I have continued to seek Him out, craving more of the spiritual food I need to sustain me and help me grow.

More importantly, I know that my Savior lives. He is my rock. Recalling the words to one of my favorite hymns says it all:

He lives! He lives! Christ Jesus lives today;
He walks with me and talks with me along
life's narrow way. He lives! He lives, salvation
to impart!

You ask me how I know he lives. He lives within
my heart.

When the Prodigal Son Comes Home

"While the son was still a long way off, his father saw him. He was filled with tender love for his son. He ran to him. He threw his arms around him and kissed him." Luke 15:20

When I opened the letter addressed to me, I wasn't expecting the words that flowed from my youngest son's heart. You see, he is my prodigal son.

Clint, who is 28-years-old, will finally graduate from Oklahoma State University this December. From the time of his birth in January 1981, he has given me joy. But he has also caused me much frustration and heartache, especially during his teen years and through his mid-twenties.

I have often said that if Clint had been my first-born, he would have been an only child. And I meant it at the time. However, God knew that I needed two sons with different personalities and gifts who would each bring me their share of joys as well as problems. My youngest child just did a better job at the second one.

As I read my son's words, the tears blurred my vision and I had to remove my glasses. Although my youngest has a delightful sense of humor, he has an uncanny ability to say the right thing at the right time. This was one of those times.

In part, he said, "When I struggled in life, you always have been there to listen and help me see why the Lord chose a certain path for me. I know they say we all have guardian angels we can't see, but I think all I have to do is look towards my mother and see mine smiling back at me."

Me, a guardian angel? I had never considered myself an angel. After all, I have made more than my share of mistakes. However, I know I am a forgiven sinner.

The final paragraph of my son's letter was a tribute, a gift that no amount of money could ever buy. He said, "They say a young man looks to marry someone like his mother and maybe that's why I'm still single, because no one can compare to you, the one who loves me unconditionally."

In probably what is the most familiar of Jesus' parables, we learn of a young son who decides to strike out on his own with his share of his father's inheritance in his possession. After spending all of the money recklessly, the prodigal son, estranged from his father, eventually returns home. He is welcomed with open arms and a celebration party where the fatted calf is prepared for a feast.

Our relationship with our heavenly Father is just like that. We may stray but when we choose to return home, He welcomes us with open arms of unconditional love.

Jesus' call to return to our Father does not end there. He calls us to mend any broken relationships that are holding us back from becoming the person whom He created us to be. Who is anxiously awaiting your return?

Praising Him in the Pain

"Not only so, but we also rejoice in our sufferings, because we know that suffering produces perseverance; perseverance, character; and character, hope. And hope does not disappoint us, because God has poured out his love into our hearts by the Holy Spirit, whom he has given us." *Romans 5:3-5*

Trying to recall the first time I ever experienced a major disappointment in my life, I thought about the time when I was around 13-years-old. I was infatuated with the newspaper delivery boy who rode his red Schwinn bicycle by my house every day to throw the evening paper into our yard. I had visions of his riding up and taking me away on his handlebars to who knows where. Of course, it never happened. Besides, I doubt we could have traveled very far with me perched so precariously.

I can look back now, laugh at some of my childhood disappointments, and thank the Lord for unanswered prayers. Life is, however, full of disappointments.

At a recent women's retreat, we heard lay speakers and pastors who spoke on a variety of topics. Speaking from their hearts, each had a life experience to share with a lesson. Some were able to speak joyfully about the work of the Lord in their lives. Others, overcome by the pain of past hurts, were able to share but not without tears.

Looking back at my own life over the last eight years, I marvel at the disappointments and struggles I have overcome because my Savior has sustained me.

Although I grew up in the church, I didn't have a personal relationship with my Creator until the end of my marriage in 2001. What followed were more disappointments, struggles with cancer, the death of my parents, a strained relationship with a close relative and the end of another relationship that I thought had a future.

As I have pondered these experiences, I realize that God has used it for my growth. Although there are times I have wanted to give up, I have persevered through the pain and heartache to feel the "peace that passes all understanding." I have learned that no matter how bad things get in life or how dark the night seems, the Lord is in control and I am never alone.

Dr. Carlfred Broderick, author of "The Uses of Adversity," wrote, "The gospel of Jesus Christ is not insurance against pain."

While some of life's trials may seem so deep that no words of comfort have meaning, we can face our soul-wrenching grief with hope. Our Savior's yoke has lightened our own load. In Psalms 18:2, the writer says, "The Lord is my rock, my fortress and my deliverer; my God is my rock, in whom I take refuge. He is my shield and the horn of my salvation, my stronghold."

God is always at work in our lives. Even though our eyes may not see nor our ears hear what is going on behind the scenes, we can still praise him in the pain, realizing that He loves us.

Never Too Old to Learn

"Wisdom is a shelter as money is a shelter, but the advantage of knowledge is this: that wisdom preserves the life of its possessor." *Ecclesiastes 7:12*

During a recent interview for an article I was writing, I was surprised when the woman said, "I'm 72-years-old but I'm still learning just like a little kid."

I not only laughed, because she did, but because it is a profound truth we sometimes forget. Just when we "think" we know it all, God has to remind us that we are but babes, still learning, still growing. We are still under construction.

At one time, I didn't want to admit that I didn't know it all. With each birthday I celebrated, I thought I was growing wiser. While age may be an indicator of growing older, it is no guarantee that you are gaining wisdom.

God has taught me many lessons since I began seeking Him and His path for my life. Proverbs 9:10 says, "If you really want to become wise, you must begin by having respect for the Lord. To know the Holy One is to gain understanding."

To know the Lord means we must spend time with Him on a daily basis in prayer and reading His Word. In our fast-paced, technologically-saturated world, we often find it challenging to carve out that time. That's why I spend time with Him every morning before my day gets hectic. It's about setting priorities. For me, a personal relationship with God is number one.

Stephen R. Covey, author of "The Seven Habits of Highly Effective People: Restoring the Character Ethic," says, "The key is not to prioritize what's on your schedule, but to schedule your priorities."

For me, scheduling priorities came with a wisdom born of failures and God's guidance. Proverbs 16:20

says, "Whoever gives heed to instruction prospers, and blessed is he who trusts in the Lord."

As I have learned to trust in the Lord with all my heart and lean not on my own understanding, He has blessed me more than I could ever deserve. I have acknowledged Him and His ways and He has made my paths straight.

When I quit worrying about tomorrow and began honoring Him with my first fruits, my life began to overflow with many blessings, including financial. When I chose to put God at the center of my life, He became the source of my security, my guidance, my power and my wisdom. That is why I have chosen to serve the Lord.

By society's standards, I had achieved much success by my late 40s. But I found myself struggling with issues, leaving me with an inner hunger and a deep need that I eventually learned could only be satisfied through a personal relationship with my Lord.

As I continue to seek His wisdom, I am amazed at how much I still don't know. Growing spiritually is not easy. In fact, it can be downright painful sometimes. I have shed many tears during what I call my growth spurts; however, God is my healer and always available to bind up the wounds.

Radically in Love

"Now that same day two of them were going to a village called Emmaus, about seven miles from Jerusalem. They were talking with each other about everything that had happened. As they talked and discussed these things with each other, Jesus himself came up and walked along with them; but they were kept from recognizing him." *Luke 24:13-16*

Imagine walking down the dusty road on that first Easter afternoon from Jerusalem to Emmaus. The two disciples, preoccupied with their own sadness and hopelessness, cannot see God's redemptive purpose in the things that led up to, and the event that occurred, on Friday.

When the risen Christ "came up and walked along with them," the two didn't recognize Him. Upon their arrival in Emmaus, He "took bread, blessed and broke it, and gave it to them." Then, their eyes were opened and the fire of God's love was ignited in their hearts.

If I had been there that afternoon, how would I have responded? Would I have been so consumed by my own grief I could not have seen through my tears to recognize the risen Savior?

I once had a person make this observation about me: "You don't cry much, do you?" Without thinking, I responded, "No."

I never thought much about that question, or my response, until several things in my life led me to my knees in prayer. I prided myself on being strong. I didn't want others to see my weaknesses, especially the tears. I have since learned that tears are healing.

In early May 2009, I participated in The Walk to Emmaus, a spiritual renewal program designed to strengthen local churches through the development of

Christian disciples and leaders. The program emphasizes Jesus as our model of servanthood.

During the 72-hour experience, we were wrapped in agape love, spent time in meditation and prayer, shared special times of worship and celebrated Holy Communion daily. For many, like me, it was a time of healing and growth.

As pilgrims on our "walk," we were on a journey to rediscover Christ's presence in our lives. I not only gained a fresh awareness of God's transforming grace but I left my walk with a deeper understanding of God's purpose for my life. While on my "walk," I formed new friendships that will help foster my faith and support my ongoing spiritual maturity.

Leaving the spiritual retreat at the end of the 72 hours was hard for me. Like others, I had been on the mountaintop of God's love. However, when we walked out the doors of the church, we were fueled with the Holy Spirit so we could share that love with a hurting world.

Before I experienced a deeper spiritual connection on the "walk," I was hurting. Like the disciples on the road to Emmaus, I was absorbed in my own sadness connected with what I thought I wanted in my life. I couldn't see that God's perfect plan was my spiritual growth so that I could be better equipped to serve Him and bear witness to the Good News. My self-centeredness was getting in the way of God's using me for His purposes.

At Sunday's closing, I stood to share my testimony about my Emmaus experience. With tears freely flowing down my face, I confessed, "I am radically in love with my Savior."

The Grace of Giving

"But just as you excel in everything—in faith, in speech, in knowledge, in complete earnestness and in your love for us —see that you also excel in this grace of giving." *2 Corinthians 8:7*

"Give us this day our daily bread" is engraved on the pewter tray that I recently gave as a housewarming gift. I had debated for over a month about presenting this tray to my friend. The gift wasn't new and it also held special meaning for me because it had belonged to my mother.

I wanted to give James and his wife something special to commemorate the purchase of their first home. It had been six months since the young couple had moved into their Tulsa residence and I had not found the right gift. They were excited and had spent many hours on the renovation of the older structure.

More than once, God had nudged me to consider giving my mother's bread tray to them. However, I kept resisting for several reasons. First, it had belonged to my mother. Second, it wasn't new. Aren't you supposed to give a brand new item as a gift?

Recently, James, whom I work with on our church magazine, was at my house helping me finish the latest edition before he left for a mission trip to Poland. Although I still wasn't sure it was the right thing to do, I presented the simple metal tray to him before he left that afternoon. His reaction to my gift let me know that I had made the right decision.

I recall a birthday gift I received from a friend about a decade ago. When she gave me the present, she said, "Carol, I almost didn't give you this bracelet because after I bought it, I wanted to keep it for myself." However, Judy, unselfishly, gave it to me.

Two years ago, I was cleaning and organizing my jewelry box when I came across the beautiful piece of jewelry. I knew how much my friend had coveted that bracelet but had chosen to give it to me instead. Since Judy's birthday is the day before mine, I decided to wrap it up and give it back to her. I had to mail it because we no longer live in the same town.

When my phone rang a few days later, I was delighted to hear Judy's voice. She was amazed at my generosity.

One of my favorite television ministers often talks about her growth as a giver. Even if the item she gives away has special meaning for her, she listens to that still small voice that urges her to give it away.

Humans are selfish by nature. Generosity does not come naturally for us but is the result of God's grace. This is what Paul is referring to when he addresses the Corinthians and encourages them to excel in giving as well.

When we realize that God's grace is more than enough, we can give generously and from the heart, even if it is a prized personal possession.

My Chains Are Gone

"All of us have sinned and fallen short of God's glory. But God treats us much better than we deserve, and because of Christ Jesus, He freely accepts us and sets us free from our sins." *Romans 3:23-24 (CEV)*

My grandchildren recently spent a Saturday night with me. I don't know what their father fed them before he dropped them off at my house but I know it must have been loaded with caffeine or sugar.

My phone rang shortly after their father's departure. As I tried to carry on a conversation, Cheyenne and Brennan decided to race throughout the house chasing my dog. Between their squealing and the dog's barking, I was having a difficult time focusing on the person at the other end of the line. After several attempts at trying to quell the noise, I ended the conversation.

Immediately, I asked my grandchildren to sit down. I explained that their behavior while I was on the phone was unacceptable. My four-year-old grandson, who is usually the first one to apologize, said, "We're sorry, Nana."

Later, the two became rambunctious again. Because it was too hot to go outdoors, I tried to find something we could do together that didn't involve bringing the roof down. Cheyenne wanted me to read a library book to her while Brennan chose to play with a toy car. After I finished reading to my granddaughter, she decided to color. However, the peace didn't last long before the two were fighting and Nana had to be the referee.

At the end of my patience, I said, "If you don't settle down, I'm going to bury you two in the backyard." Of course, I wasn't serious but Brennan wasn't sure. He said, "Nana, you wouldn't do that, would you?"

With a grin on my face, I said, "What do you think?" My smile gave way to laughter when my grandson said, "I don't think so."

Through this exchange with my grandchildren, I can understand how frustrated our Heavenly Father must get with us when we disobey Him. Like children, we sometimes race through life ignoring the warnings He gives us until He has to get our attention.

I recall those times when I have disregarded God's nudges until He had to hit me over the head to get my attention. It wasn't pleasant.

For too many years though, I carried a burden of guilt instead of asking for His forgiveness. It wasn't until I came to accept His amazing grace that I was set free.

One of my favorite hymns says it all,

"Amazing grace, how sweet the sound that saved a wretch like me. I once was lost, but now I'm found, was blind, but now I see. 'Twas grace that taught my heart to fear and grace my fears relieved. How precious did that grace appear the hour I first believed. My chains are gone, I've been set free. My God, my Savior has ransomed me and like a flood, His mercy rains, unending love, Amazing grace."

God's Perfect Global Positioning System

"And now, O Israel, what does the Lord your God ask of you but to fear the Lord your God, to walk in all his ways, to love him, to serve the Lord your God with all your heart and with all your soul, and to observe the Lord's commands and decrees that I am giving you today for your own good?" *Deuteronomy 10:12-13*

Going down a one-way street—the wrong way—is not only dangerous, but also terrifying, especially if you are the passenger. I wasn't. I was the driver and I was 17-years-old the first time my parents let me drive out-of-town without adult supervision.

I was enrolling in a junior college located 45 minutes from home. My sister and a friend had ridden along to keep me company. After completing enrollment, I decided to check out the small town. I didn't have much driving experience. I had delayed getting my driver's license at the usual age of 16 because I was afraid of failing the parallel parking portion of the test. Eventually, I mustered the courage to try and lucked out because the testing officer didn't require me to park between two vehicles. I only had to park behind one. Otherwise, I know I would have failed or hit one of the cars in the process.

The day of my first college enrollment found me confident behind the wheel until I overlooked the one-way street sign that found us traveling head-on against oncoming traffic. My sister freaked. So did my friend. Somehow, I managed to maneuver the automobile onto the sidewalk and into a nearby parking lot. Looking back now, I can laugh at my inexperience. It wasn't funny at the time.

For Christmas, I received a GPS. It is not something I would have purchased for myself, even though I have a terrible sense of direction. As I was discussing the GPS with a friend, she mentioned a sermon she had heard. While using his GPS, the pastor decided to ignore the directions given by the mechanical voice. Each time he did, the "voice" would remind him that he was going the wrong way. As he continued to disobey the orders to "turn here," the voice became less insistent and eventually gave up trying to redirect his path. When the pastor finally decided to turn on a familiar street, the GPS began to respond again.

Our relationship with God can be just like this. Sometimes we're so focused on going our way, we can't hear God's voice trying to redirect us or trying to stop us from making a wrong turn. Maybe it's a direction that we're determined to go in or a path that we've chosen to make things happen, no matter what anyone thinks, even God.

Each time we ignore God and continue driving full speed ahead, we become lost. Although He allows U-turns, we have to tune in to His global positioning system on a daily basis to drive in the direction He wants us to go. Are you following His voice?

Living Life to the Full

"The thief comes only to steal, kill and destroy. I have come that they may have life and have it to the full." *John 10:10*

As a child, I could wile away the hours on a lazy summer afternoon by hiding in the branches of a Mimosa tree or lying on a carpet of clover, looking for the elusive one with four leaves. Recalling those days makes me smile because I now understand why I could spend those hours alone and yet not feel lonely.

That understanding has also led to a deeper one. We are born with a desire, a nagging sense of destiny, that there is more to life than what our eyes can see and our ears can hear.

Like many adults in our society, I became caught up in proving to others and myself that my life was about a list of accomplishments and accolades. As a teacher, I enjoyed the recognition that came when my students won awards in journalism competitions. In 1992, after our newspaper garnered the highest state award possible for a high school publication, I was surprised by my reaction. I felt nothing but emptiness.

While I was not aware at the time of what was happening inside my soul, I believe it was the first step that God used to draw me back to Him. That year, I left the classroom and took another position in the same school system where I stayed for another 13 years until God led me on a different path.

As I reflect on the journey He has me on, I can further understand His plan and purpose for my life. By focusing on God, I have learned to say "No" to those things that do not further His kingdom. I have also become aware of what gifts He has called me to use and when to politely decline when I am asked to do something, even if it is within my capabilities.

Og Mandino, author of the bestselling book "The Greatest Salesman in the World," once said, "You are not the momentary whim of a careless creator experimenting in the laboratory of life. . . You were made with a purpose."

During my 20s and 30s, I looked everywhere, but to my Creator, to find that "something" that would fill that God-shaped hole in me. I had this nagging suspicion that there was a plan but I was trying too hard to make it work without consulting the One who has a better blueprint for my life.

In John 10:10, Jesus says that He has come so that we might have life and have it to the full. In Eugene Peterson's translation, Jesus says, "I came so they can have real and eternal life, more and better life than they ever dreamed of."

As I have come to enjoy an abundant life through my Savior, I know it is the simple that makes life worthwhile. Recently, I was lying on the grass looking at the night sky with my grandchildren. As we counted the stars, I also counted my blessings.

Meet the Author

If anyone is surprised by the paths that God has led her on, it is Carol Round. Although she has seen success in other areas of her life as a former teacher, professional photographer and freelance writer, she never envisioned herself as a columnist, especially a faith-based columnist.

But God had other plans for her life. Carol's columns take an honest, and sometimes humorous, look at the struggles we all have with fears, uncertainty, self-esteem and relationships, as well as life's joys and surprises. "A Matter of Faith," her self-syndicated column, currently runs in 12 Oklahoma newspapers and *Capper's*, a national publication with a circulation of over 200,000.

Carol's feature stories, essays, poetry and photos have appeared in *American Profile* magazine, *Western Horseman*, *Plus* magazine, *Oklahoma* magazine, *Ozark Mountaineer*, the *Don't Sweat the Small Stuff* anthology series, *Raging Gracefully* and *Hometown Heroes*.

She is the mother of two grown sons, grandmother to Cheyenne and Brennan, and obedient owner to a spoiled dog named Taco. Carol resides in Claremore, Oklahoma, where she retired after 30 years as a high school teacher.

Contact the Author

I would love to hear from you. If you have read one of my weekly columns or one of my book collections and it has touched your life in some way, please email me at **carolaround@yahoo.com** or by snail mail at 1521 Pheasant Circle, Claremore, OK 74019.

I always love hearing from my readers. It is affirmation that I am following God's leading by using my writing gift to glorify Him.

In His Grip,

Carol

Breinigsville, PA USA
27 October 2009
226505BV00001B/5/P

9 780937 660836